Thoughts That Harm Thoughts That Heal

OVERCOMING COMMON AILMENTS THROUGH THE **POWER OF YOUR MIND**

KEITH MASON

PIATKUS

The data supplied in this book is for your personal information only. It does not replace the advice of your doctor or professional therapist whom you should always consult if you are suffering from any form of illness or if you have sustained an accident. The author does not seek to advise on appropriate specific action and can accept no responsibility for actions taken by readers based upon the contents of this book which may result in: (a) physical or mental injury or mental and emotional stress to themselves or any third party; or (b) any loss of any description, economic or otherwise, as a result of following the advice in this book.

Copyright © 2000 by Keith Mason

Published in the UK in 2000 by
Judy Piatkus (Publishers) Limited
5 Windmill Street
London W1P 1HF
e-mail: info@piatkus.co.uk

**For the latest news and information on all our titles, visit
our website at www.piatkus.co.uk**

The moral rights of the author have been asserted

A catalogue record for this book is available from the British Library

ISBN 0-7499-2078-5

Design by Paul Saunders
Edited by Kelly Davis

Typeset by Phoenix Photosetting, Chatham, Kent
Printed and bound in Great Britain by
Biddles Ltd, Guildford & King's Lynn
www.biddles.co.uk

CONTENTS

INTRODUCTION

Have you ever wondered how your body knows how to heal a cut finger, or repair a sports injury or a twisted ankle? Ever noticed how when you get stressed you immediately feel that knot of tension in your stomach? And what of those times when you've eaten something unwholesome and, almost immediately, you start to feel physically ill?

Medical science explains these phenomena using convoluted and perplexing terminology ('it's all to do with biological functions and chemical reactions'), while physicists speak of atoms, electrons and photons, and mystify us even more. Well, I believe it's time for a more commonsense approach – one that we can all understand and use to improve our own health and that of our friends and families.

After more than twenty-five years of practical experience in complementary healthcare, I know that the mind exerts enormous power over the body. I am also convinced that many chronic and serious illnesses have their origins in the harm people do themselves due to worry and anxiety. Negative attitudes to life and to the people around us can cause stress and tension that weaken our general constitution, compromise our immune system, and allow the invasion of viruses and bacteria, which can trigger more serious illnesses.

It is in fact very difficult for the body to be sick. Believe it or not, it's always striving for perfection. So, why shouldn't we consciously assist our general constitution and immune system, and treat our bodies to some healing thoughts – instead of those that harm? Sounds fanciful? Well, as you will see, there is now actual evidence to show what types of thoughts harm which area of the body, and which thoughts heal. There are also mental stress management techniques that you can learn in order to reduce or eliminate the physical symptoms.

This book is in two sections. Part One deals with the basic make-up of the body, and examines how natural information passes through the central nervous system, and from cell to cell, to correct ill-health. This first part of the book explains why our thoughts and attitudes affect our mental and emotional states along with our physical bodies. It also shows how these thoughts and attitudes can maintain a state of well-being or, alternatively, a state of illness.

Part Two lists the most common physical ailments from A to Z, along with some familiar mental and emotional conditions. To assist the reader, there is a brief summary under each heading explaining the main symptoms, and in some cases what conventional therapy may be offered. For each ailment, the thoughts and attitudes that can cause the condition are described. Likewise, attitudes and mental stress management techniques that will assist in the healing of the condition are explained, as well as the relevant complementary remedies.

Thoughts That Harm, Thoughts That Heal will be helpful to practitioners of both orthodox and complementary therapies and to all patients interested in attaining optimum health. In any illness, the correct attitude of mind can only help in the healing process, irrespective of what other treatment the patient is receiving.

Part One

The Mind–Body Connection

'Before medical researchers can expect a breakthrough in their unending search for the causes of illness in humanity, they must first understand the purpose and cause of the human form. It is this understanding that will bring relief to the suffering, as to know the true cause and purpose of the human form is to know the cause of illness.'

Keith Mason

'A symptom that has been created and then manifests itself in the body can be similarly uncreated or destroyed. All one needs is the belief and strength of mind to summon up the courage to search within and find the adversary deep inside that resulted in the illness; this is the real challenge and often the harder to accept.'

Chrissie Mason

Chapter One

A More Natural Approach

W̲E SAT IN SILENCE – my wife Chrissie and I, together, in the back of a London cab. A black shell of gloom encapsulated us, yet the hustle and bustle of the outside world continued, oblivious to the shattering news we had just received. Chrissie turned to me: 'Do you truly believe in what you say, in what you tell your patients and what you lecture and write about?'

Before I could even answer she looked at me again, this time with a sudden return of the old glint in her eye. I sensed a lightening of my own personal gloom. 'Yes, I do,' was my reply.

'Then we will use a totally natural approach to change the present state of my health,' she replied. As she finished the sentence we both smiled. That journey in a London cab had only just started, yet it began an exploration that continues to this very day. Chrissie's illness is now a mere memory, but it played a central part in a journey that has taken us all over the world, from the USA to Australia and Europe, learning and exchanging views on complementary medicine and how to deal with chronic illness.

We decided there and then, all those years ago, no more dread of the big C. And no more fear when doctors in white coats say:

'I am afraid it's cancer.' Fear is the most powerful emotion affecting humanity, especially when it comes to chronic illness.

But who really feels the most fear? The doctor, who knows that, with the relatively ineffectual healing tools at his disposal, there's little he can do to help the patient's symptoms? Or the patient, receiving the diagnosis and being fearful of the eventual consequences, due to the stigma attached to a certain illness?

From the orthodox perspective there was little that could be done for Chrissie. Certainly the doctors held no hope for the future; in their opinion there wasn't even any point in reviewing the prognosis. But defeat simply wasn't on the agenda for Chrissie or me. The answer had to lie within us – we had to change the way the cells in her body were behaving. And we had to find out how and why such an illness could take hold, as, even in those early days of complementary medicine, we considered ourselves reasonably well informed and had always tried to follow a healthy, nutritious diet.

This was how our researches and investigations began, eventually leading to the creation of the database of information that has enabled me to write this book. It started eighteen years ago, back in 1982, when Chrissie was diagnosed with cancer. At this point, I had already been in alternative medical practice in South Africa for some twelve years, using homeopathy, radionics and naturopathic medicine. At that time White's Chemist in Cape Town (renowned for its stocks of herbs, homeopathic and flower essence remedies, and not for treating whites only as the name might imply in a country that was then in the grip of apartheid) was a regular meeting place for practitioners of complementary medicine.

It was in Africa that I first encountered the extraordinary effects of homeopathic remedies, and the way flower essences could ease the symptoms of severe illness and the stresses experienced in that country by both the black and white populations. My African patients loved the herbal remedies in particular – the more loathsome the taste, the better the effect. I witnessed recoveries from inveterate diseases and the healing of chronic illness by the use of nature's own remedies and by correcting the nutrition of patients. It was also in Cape Town that I first met practitioners of radionics, a therapy based on traditional wisdom, which analysed the cause of a set of symptoms and took account of emotional and mental factors in the creation of illness.

In addition, I observed how certain sets of symptoms were more prevalent in certain types of patient personalities and realised that people's attitudes had a profound effect on the final outcome of their illness. The actions of the patient's mind appeared to influence both acute and chronic illness, and in many cases the mental attitude seemed to act more therapeutically than the remedies administered.

'Let the body heal itself'

So it was that eighteen years ago I found myself back in England, practising in London, at the Institute for Complementary Medicine, and facing the biggest challenge of my career. I was going to have to use the skills and philosophical beliefs I had acquired in order to save the most precious person in my world.

Certainly conventional medicine had failed us, and a more natural approach was needed. But it had to be a joint effort, as the person who would make the real difference was Chrissie herself. It wasn't just her own will to live, her personality or her mental and emotional strengths, but the very cells within her body and the life force contained within those cells – that's what did the healing. We knew it, we discussed it at length and decided on this joint natural approach.

'Let the body heal itself,' Chrissie said. 'It knows what to do. It created the problem, it can fix the problem, for it's far more intelligent than you or me.' Never has a truer word been said.

I had always believed there was a need for a more natural approach to healing but that it should be based upon solid foundations, using both physiological and psychological principles for diagnosis and treatment. For years I had been convinced that 'knowingness', a form of intelligence, existed in each and every cell of the human body.

Cells actually *know* what to do; they have a purpose, a role to play, in the running of all our bodily functions. But, to me, their most incredible attribute is their ability to reproduce and replicate themselves exactly.

For instance, think about what happens when you meet a friend in the street whom you've not seen for more than six months. Take a good look at them . . . They are different from when you last saw them. They may look the same at first glance, they may have aged a little, but they are essentially new. Since you last saw them a few months ago, all the cells of their body have replicated themselves. The cells of the eyes renew themselves every few days; skin cells after a few weeks; nerve and bone cells in about six months. Our bodies are in a continual state of renewal and replication.

So why, we may ask, does any illness last more than six months? And why don't these cells that are reproduced from the old cells become totally healthy, given that the body knows what to do in terms of cell reproduction and self-preservation? In addition, we should consider what effect the mind has upon the body and how the power of thought, both positive and negative, will affect the performance of the cells and the entire body.

However, there is an additional factor to take into consideration, and this applies to both healthy and unhealthy people: the human body and its cells must have a purpose. To effect a cure from any illness, all patients must have a purpose in their lives, and this included my wife all those years ago. In addition, the little cells that can heal and reproduce healthy cells must also share that purpose; it's a mind–body thing. If someone loses sight of their own purpose in life, the cells that make up their body will have no purpose and there will be no requirement for their existence to carry out bodily functions. Illness will then proliferate.

I remember the words of the late Dr Aubrey Westlake, my mentor, who also practised in his earlier years in London with Dr Bach of flower essence fame. He said something I will never forget: '*All illness is curable, but not all patients.*' In my thirty years of complementary medical practice this has been proved to me so many times. Patients have come to me with chronic, so-called incurable illnesses, yet they had the will and a purpose for which to live and they did; while others have come with lesser illnesses that should have responded readily to either conventional or complementary medicine and yet they died.

Cause and effect

So, eighteen years ago, I came to the conclusion that my diagnostic approach to healing had to change because the power of the mind and the person's thoughts had a direct bearing upon the outcome of their illness. This strategy goes beyond mere positive thinking; it is based on a complete assessment of a patient's illness, physical, mental and emotional, along with the establishment of a cause for a set of symptoms. Treating the observable symptoms a patient displays, whether by conventional or complementary therapy, is not enough. Medical practice must discover the cause before it can expect to cure the symptoms.

The law of cause and effect exists throughout the world of nature and applies equally to medicine and to the human body. No set of symptoms appears randomly; there has to be an underlying reason or cause for those symptoms to manifest. Apart from genetic and hereditary factors, stress, trauma and anxiety are some of the most common causes of illness. In other words, the mind affects the performance of the body and the cells within the body.

Poor nutrition, prescribed drugs, mechanical injury, surgical procedures and general abuse of the body with addictive substances may cause further damage. Combine all these factors with the stresses of life in modern society and we find the reasons for so much illness in the world staring us in the face.

So, when Chrissie and I faced the challenge of the diagnosis she had received, we had to step back and take stock of both the physical and mental aspects of our lives. We knew our diets were adequate and we both took regular vitamin supplements to aid our immune response and our general constitutions. We took some time to look at our stress levels; these seemed no worse than others in our profession experienced. We looked for anxieties or worries that affected our lives and questioned one another intently, trying to establish whether any other stress or trauma was affecting Chrissie's life in particular. We could think of nothing. We certainly had purpose in our lives, we had healthy children and careers we enjoyed, so what was preventing the replication of healthy cells in Chrissie's body?

We looked at family history, and here we found our first lead, as Chrissie's grandmother, mother and two of her sisters had all experienced gynaecological problems (the same physical area now affected in Chrissie), so there seemed to be a genetic factor. Before receiving the final, devastating diagnosis, Chrissie had already been taking all the right remedies and supplements for the generative organs, as this was the location of the symptoms, yet still the illness proliferated. There had to be more to it; something that was imprisoned within the cells was inhibiting healthy cell replication. We had to identify this negative force.

It was at this stage that we turned to our dear friend and colleague, spiritual healer Betty Shine. Betty not only gave Chrissie healing but also hypnosis. To this day, we believe it was the depth of the hypnosis and Betty's subtle, psychic probing into

Chrissie's subconscious mind that finally released the negative force in the cells.

A few weeks after the hypnosis Chrissie called me to her bedside. She was emotional and yet very calm as she told me that I was the first person in the world to know that she had suffered a serious emotional trauma as a little girl. She shared the past event with me, recalling also her guilt at the time despite her very young age. She had intentionally hidden the incident away, removed it from her conscious mind, and in so doing had somehow also concealed it from her subconscious. This was a turning point and from that moment on Chrissie gained weight, colour returned to her face, and she could manage the bathroom alone. She was on the mend, and the imprisoned negative force locked away for so many years had been released. The prescribed remedies had more therapeutic effect and Chrissie gradually got well.

Releasing the 'bad guys'

Each cell in the body is actually a minute cavity or compartment containing a small mass of protoplasm with a nucleus as its core, all surrounded by a membrane. The core of the cell and the protoplasm (the essential viscid and translucent material) contain all the information needed for reproduction and self-replication. They also hold the stress and trauma suffered during each cell's relatively short life and pass this on to the daughter cell in the replication process.

Cells are aptly named, as they imprison both negative and positive information. Unfortunately, human cells keep both the good guys and the bad guys in the same 'lock-up'. If we are to have any chance of healing (or rehabilitation) in the body we have to separate them and get rid of the bad guys. The good guys speak for the whole population of cells, trying to keep the body healthy, but the bad guys in the lock-up perpetuate the bad memories from the past and they must be exterminated. Harsh words perhaps, but if the negative cell memory is not removed, illness will persist. And if a cell of the body can create illness, then it must be able to un-create it. Furthermore, remedies (whether orthodox or complementary) will only work if the negative thought is released from its imprisonment within the cell.

Another obstacle for patients in their efforts to get well is the apprehension they experience when their illness is diagnosed. The image of orthodox medicine has become tarnished in recent years. People no longer trust doctors implicitly. And the obscure vocabulary of the medical profession only confuses and frightens patients and their families. We need to start examining the cause of illness in a language we can all understand. It's time orthodox medicine came down from its erudite perch and learnt to communicate with mere mortals. If we can give patients a better understanding of what is actually happening within their bodies, and at the same time allow the friends and families that look after them the same competence, then it stands to reason that an increased number of patients are going to attain a state of well-being.

Chapter Two

STARTING ANEW

W E NEED AN understanding of how we develop from a single cell at conception in order to shed light on the power within the mind of all our cells. When conception occurs the female egg is fertilised by the male sperm and the embryo formed is little more than a large single cell. That's where we all came from – just one cell. To me this has to be the most amazing feat of nature.

The miracle of life

As you sit now, reading this book, take a few moments to marvel at yourself. Take a look at your hands holding the book, waggle your fingers, move your legs and toes, and notice how your body can exercise control through the nervous system.

Think of the day gone by or the day yet to come; think of your life and your integration with others; just take some time to realise how amazing you really are. As a human being, you literally comprise of billions of cells, each little cell a living organism alongside all the other millions within your whole body structure. And each cell has its own 'mind' and knows what to do in your body. All these cells, with differing purposes, differing abilities and roles to play in your body, all came from that one fertilised cell.

At conception that single cell started to organise itself; it divided into two, and then four, and so on, until it reached thirty-two cells. Then your individual blueprint began to emerge. From then on, the cells continued to organise themselves into outer tissues that formed the placenta and the inner mass that became you, the embryo proper. At this stage you began to implant on to your mother's uterine wall, and, after nine months, you ended up as a tiny baby destined to develop further into the adult you see today.

As you contemplate the structure of your body (the skin cells, the soft tissue cells, the nervous system and bony structure, and how it all developed into billions of cells from that one fertilised egg), ask yourself: what conscious part did you play in its growth and development? Be truthful now. Consider the question carefully. The answer has to be: none − it all happened by itself.

A mind of their own

The cells of your body way back then, and most certainly today, have a mind of their own in order to control the functions that maintain you in a state of well-being. (Remember, your body always wants to be well and perform at its optimum level.) Of course, you also have a personality and free will that can consciously direct your body to perform physical tasks and make mental and emotional demands for your interaction with your fellow human beings. But over the actual maintenance and restructuring of your body during life, the self-repair and self-reproduction processes, you have no conscious dominion. The body has a mind of its own. It knows what to do.

For instance, if you injure yourself in the garden you don't consciously intend to send cells to coagulate the blood at the site of the wound and nowhere else in your body; you don't panic and think to yourself: 'I hope the blood doesn't start clotting in my heart valves.' The body just gets on and does the required job, and only at the appropriate location.

Likewise, your immune cells appear to counter infection, and your skin begins to grow (if you could film this event through a time-lapse camera it would be amazingly fast) to close over the wound and then stop. The skin cells provide a protective layer, formed in conjunction with the coagulated blood, which in turn forms the scab.

Clearly, cells know what to do to accomplish healing, but they also know a lot more. For example, long-term changes can be made in the body to compensate for the many challenges we face throughout life. Thus the body will adapt to changes in diet, environment, stress and anxiety; it will identify poisons and toxins, along with bacteria and viruses; it will recognise any aggressor and instantly activate an army of defence cells. In addition it provides us with an adrenaline-boosting 'flight or fight mechanism' when we are under threat.

But there are times when this innate ability fails, illness takes hold, and our cells lose their ability to heal and protect us. This is what must be examined, not only by the doctor or healthcare practitioner, but by the patient themself. There has to be a reason or special cause why you become ill and your cells fail to perform their allotted task.

A quantum leap

Conventional medicine uses two main philosophies, biology and chemistry, as the basis for its treatment procedures. However, the most important philosophy, which controls the functioning of all living matter, including the human body, is physics, particularly quantum physics (the study of minute particles).

According to physicists, the atoms of all matter are held together by electromagnetic force, a theory known as quantum electro dynamics (QED). It is like an orchestrated dance, in which electrically charged particles orbit a central nucleus. This is sometimes called an electromagnetic field, and one could compare it to a miniature version of our solar system, where the planets orbit the sun in a stable, unending, yet systematic manner. This harmonic dance of atoms and electrons goes on inside every cell of the human body.

Having identified the cells that make up our physical bodies, we can break down the cells even further to the atoms that make up their structure, which are surrounded by fields of electromagnetic forces. We are all therefore composed of atoms and molecules which require electrons to move in orbit around a central nucleus. This is true of all the stable elemental complexes and compounds that make up the structure of our cells and the body as a whole.

This electromagnetic field theory is so important, because the interactions of electrons with one another and with electromagnetic radiation determine almost everything that exists in the world around us. This includes us as well as the animal and vegetable kingdoms. And it doesn't just apply to physical phenomena. Thought can also be measured in terms of electromagnetic energy – as brainwaves. This is how incorrect thought patterns can affect the performance of the fields of energy around cells and thus enhance or disable them.

To achieve a true understanding of human life and its requirements when diseased, medicine should study all three philosophies: biology, chemistry and quantum physics. Doctors would then have a much deeper knowledge of the origins of life, wellbeing and health; and orthodox medicine would certainly be more competent and qualified to heal the sick.

The elements of life

In addition to these three philosophies, doctors would benefit a great deal from studying the elements. It's worth remembering that the planet earth comprises 103 basic elements. These elements are the building blocks of all living matter – including human beings, animals, plants and the very ground on which we stand. They make up the food we eat and the fabric of our planet.

Scientists have observed how these known elements combine to form compounds and then go on to create the structures of cells, organ systems, and whatever form the living organism may eventually take. These living compounds and complexes are created by the behaviour of electrons, but the process is conducted entirely by the elements themselves.

Of course, we mere mortals cannot create a living being by throwing together a mixture of basic elements and their attendant electrons. Even the cloning of Dolly the sheep required an existing egg, made up of nature's elements and an existing DNA; and after fertilisation it had to be implanted in a living creature's womb. All cloning procedures rely entirely upon existing natural structures.

As an example, let's take a brief look at two gas elements, hydrogen and oxygen. They have a natural inclination to form water (H_2O) and, if climatic conditions are suitable, they will form ice. In the world of nature gases can become liquids, and liquids can become solids. But are the elements and their natural inclinations themselves influenced by another dimension of activity, some form of elemental intelligence that plays an integral part in the healing processes we are trying to understand?

As I have already explained, it is very difficult for the body to develop illness. It has an innate longing for well-being and its cells always endeavour to maintain our health, without our conscious intervention. So why do things go wrong? What causes a healthy individual to become unwell?

Although many people experience inherited illness or malfunctions acquired at birth, there are, in my opinion, very few basic causes of ill-health. Even those who suffer from acquired or genetic malfunctions will experience a degree of improvement from some positive, corrective thinking. This is because thought is electrical, and the cells of the body contain elemental compounds comprising electromagnetic fields of force. Taking elemental mineral supplements, known to help form healthy cells and body structures, will therefore also enhance the ability of malformed or genetically affected parts of the body to act in a more natural manner. The degree of improvement gained by taking elemental minerals and changing thought patterns will depend on the extent of the existing malfunction of the cell's DNA, which controls the cell's ability to grow and divide.

A similar principle is applied in reverse in chemotherapy, where cytotoxic chemicals prevent cells (both cancerous and healthy) from growing and dividing by damaging their genetic material. In contrast, supplying the correct biochemical elements will assist the natural development of cells.

The real causes of disease

Medical dictionaries contain thousands of named diseases, but these are no more than categorised sets of symptoms observed over many years and often named after the observer. The description of each disease may be meticulously detailed but there is never any mention of its cause.

I came across a wonderful example of this recently. A patient had been told he had 'orthostatic dysplasia'. Mystified, he had asked the consultant to write it down. What does this mean? asked the very worried patient during our consultation. I referred him to my medical dictionary and a smile spread across his face when he read 'difficulty in breathing when in the standing position'.

Another alarming-sounding disease is 'seborrheic dermatitis' which actually just means inflamed and itchy skin. Or what about Moebius disease, named after the eminent doctor who observed this set of symptoms? If you have just had this diagnosed for you, you probably have no idea how serious it is. Actually it simply means headaches or migraines that affect the muscles of the eyes. As you can see, none of this medical jargon relates at all to the cause of the condition. Many patients become bewildered by the complicated description given to their illness, when really they simply want to know how the illness originated, how it is likely to develop, and what can be done to cure it.

In my opinion most illness can be ascribed to five main causal categories: (apart from those classified as genetic or inherited):

- **1 Detrimental substances taken into the body**, including prescribed and recreational drugs, insecticides and pesticides, poisons and other ingested materials (such as food additives and colourings).
- **2 Nutrient deficiencies** due to eating poor-quality and processed foods which provide inadequate supplies of minerals and vitamins.
- **3 Mechanical injury** caused by accident or surgical intervention.
- **4 Environmental or exterior stress**, due to professional and social pressures, and having to work and live in an environment for which the human body was not designed, as well as bombardment by microwave and electrical activity.
- **5 Inner stress**, due to inability to express oneself, negative repercussions from inappropriate attitudes to others, the effects of other people's convictions and demands, along with jealousy, worry, anxiety and general mental and emotional upset.

All five categories, if ignored, will eventually lead to illness. And a more immediate problem is that all these factors will lower the immune system and the general constitution of patients. With a compromised immune system, patients will succumb more easily to invading bacteria and viruses.

Taking in drugs and toxins

The first category of causes includes the use (or overuse) of prescribed drugs, a problem that more enlightened GPs are now recognising. Without wishing to cast aspersions on orthodox medicine, one can't help wondering about the logic of recommending drugs that require continuous repeat prescriptions year after year. Most, if not all, prescription drugs have known side-effects, from which the patient is bound to suffer.

As a practitioner of complementary medicine, my patients would soon complain if I prescribed a natural remedy year after year and the symptoms continued, albeit in a controlled manner. Eventually I would have no patients left; yet many people will take conventional drugs year after year without a word of complaint to the prescribing physician – something I find quite bemusing.

Many orthodox drugs work by altering the action of naturally occurring enzymes in the body. For example, liver enzymes stimulate the breakdown of nutrients and help digest food. Drugs use these liver enzymes for their absorption and in so doing alter the naturally occurring functions in the body. (In other words, the innate ability of the cell to do its job naturally is irreversibly altered by the drug.) Once cells that perform a major role in the nutrition and digestive processes are chemically altered by drugs, they become detrimental foreign substances that the body cannot deal with.

It was the Nobel Prizewinner Linus Pauling who used the phrase 'Orthomolecular Medicine' to describe the use of the right molecules, in the correct amounts, in the right areas of the body, to heal disease. Chemical drugs are not such substances.

The body does not know how to deal with forcibly administered chemicals. When drugs are used by doctors for years on end
to control but not cure their patients' conditions, we are forced to
ask whether the massive incomes derived from repeat prescriptions may be a factor. Certainly there seems to be a lack of consideration for the patient suffering the controlled side-effects. Do the
interests of shareholders perhaps take precedence over patient care?

Recreational drugs have similar effects upon the body, as do
the residues of poisons, insecticides and pesticides in our food
(including the antibiotics and steroids used in farming). The
continual ingestion of these substances weakens our immune
systems and general well-being, but not of course the health of
the industrialists' bank balances.

We take in many other insidious materials that cause illness,
such as the toxins from the metal fillings used by the dental
profession. I should add that not everyone suffers toxicity from
their amalgam fillings but over many years I have witnessed
improvement in a number of patients after amalgam removal.
However, a word of warning here: the process of removing the
fillings may lead to a temporary increase in mercury absorption,
as bits of filling may be inadvertently chipped off and swallowed.
It is therefore best not to have amalgam fillings removed during
pregnancy or while breast-feeding.

I recall a patient named Hilary, who had been treated with
antibiotics for cystitis, inflammation of the urinary tract and
bladder for over five years. The condition would not heal and, as
is often the case, she had been told by her doctor that nothing
more could be done and she just had to live with it. The antibiotics caused major problems with her digestive system and
liver, and eventually a visit to an alternative medical practitioner
was suggested. It was a classic case of detrimental substances in
the body – the residue from the antibiotic and its alteration of
natural liver enzyme activity, as well as toxic effects from atoms
of mercury slowly leaking from her amalgam fillings.

There are many symptoms related to amalgam toxicity, including frequent headaches, gum disorders and gastro-intestinal disorders with a typical loose bowel. It affects the skin and, if evident for prolonged periods as a toxin in the blood, can cause malignancy.

I treated Hilary with both homeopathic remedies and mineral supplements to restore the cell structures of the urinary tract and bladder disrupted by the infiltration of incorrect elemental structures. I also advised her to have her amalgam fillings removed. In addition I gave her the positive thoughts and attitudes required for optimum function of her urinary tract. These would help her develop more confidence in her decision-making and take more control of events in her business and personal life, rather than be influenced by the strong convictions of others.

She admitted to me that for years she had been lacking in self-confidence and this probably stemmed from a difficult childhood. The combination of these thoughts and the remedies healed the affected cell structures and the symptoms. When Heather introduced another patient to me, a few years later, she was still free of symptoms.

Interestingly, amalgam filling material (a mixture of mercury, silver and other elements), when placed in a patient's tooth, can sometimes cause a process called electrolysis. This is the procedure used in electroplating, when rods of dissimilar metals are placed in a bath of liquid and an electric current is passed between the two. The same can happen in the mouth: with the dissimilar metals being the amalgam filling material, the bath of liquid being the saliva, and the naturally occurring electricity being provided by our body cells (many of us experience static electricity that sparks as we take off clothes).

When electrolysis occurs, the metal filling material gives off atoms of silver and mercury. These enter the digestive system and pass through the glands, causing a toxic reaction. Filling material suddenly breaks up and falls out of the tooth, not from the continual pressure of chewing but from the electrolysis process in the mouth. Again, the body cannot tolerate these toxins and poisonous atoms and it falls sick. A metallic taste, almost like tasting blood in your mouth, is one of the signs of metal toxicity. There is also a test available to confirm the presence of mercury. For information on this, contact the Holistic Dental Association (see Useful Addresses).

It is obvious that taking in harmful, foreign substances affects our cells' ability to control functions we depend upon for maintaining our well-being. The electromagnetic field created by the toxic substance causes adverse reactions with the naturally occurring fields of force around our cells. It is as if dancers on a stage were performing to different musical scores; chaos would be the result.

Other causes of disease

I have dealt with the first category of illness in some detail, as it has such a profound effect upon health, but so does the second – nutrient deficiencies. A healthy diet is essential for the maintenance of well-being and optimum health. Yet nutrition is sadly neglected by many physicians and seems to be largely absent from their medical training. It is therefore not surprising that many conventional doctors are hesitant about giving nutritional advice, as it is frequently a subject of which they have little knowledge. However, the basic principles of good nutrition are relatively simple and should be known by general practitioners. Most complementary medicine practitioners, by contrast, irrespective of their particular area of expertise, include questions on nutrition as a normal part of their initial assessment of the patient.

Nutrition actually plays a vital role in patients' welfare. In Part

Two of this book (An A-Z of Mental, Emotional and Physical Ailments) I list, where appropriate, those vitamins and minerals that will aid healing and in some cases what foods they are contained in.

The third category of illness is that caused by mechanical injury, accident or surgical intervention. In such cases treatment aims to restore the integrity of the human form to the best levels possible, according to the seriousness of the physical malfunction. The main priority in such conditions is to give patients more tolerance of the situation in which they find themselves. They also need goals and ambitions, based upon the anticipated parameters of their abilities, in whatever career or pastime they enjoy.

The forth and fifth categories of illness, caused by inner and outer stress, are the ones that respond most successfully to the approach described in this book. My own research has led me to the conclusion that about 85 per cent of illnesses in the Western world are stress-induced. Doctors may diagnose immune deficiency, or chronic bowel or digestive problems, along with skin conditions and perhaps asthma and endocrine insufficiencies, but the primary cause often comes down to stress.

Illness in patients comes about for known reasons – it *always* has a cause. Find and treat that cause and the illness has no further ground on which to proliferate. Identify the stress, change the attitudes, and well-being will result. It's not as difficult as you may think – it's actually quite elementary.

Chapter Three

IT'S ALL ELEMENTARY

S CIENTISTS TELL us that fifteen billion years ago a momentous explosion took place. This 'big bang' caused a dynamic and continuing state of expansion in the universe, which can still be measured and observed today and enables us to predict its age and constituents. Fifteen billion years! The idea of that amount of time (in comparison to the very brief period we spend here on earth) is so difficult to grasp.

All we can do, as mere mortals, is accept the explanations of the scientists and look at the structures of our bodies in the manner they suggest. So, did we all evolve from a carbon-based intelligent life form that is still in a dynamic state of evolution? The passage of time can only be examined by looking in depth at the very earth we stand upon. The fossil record shows that all living species did not come into existence at the same time; there are chronological steps, from bacteria and algae to large inverte-brates, fishes, amphibians, reptiles, birds, mammals and finally man. The complex phenomenon we call 'life', and all that we can observe, within and around us, is based on elements derived from the carbon-based organic chemicals that emanated from that big bang billions of years ago.

All life is therefore based upon chemical elements and these include the solid, liquid and gas elements of which our physical bodies are constructed and upon which we rely for our nourishment. So it's all elementary; the elements make up the chemistry and the chemistry makes up the organs and the total structure of tissues and bones of the human form.

The strange properties of elements

If we are to take more responsibility for our own health then it is important to know a little about the make-up of our bodies and the role the elements and minerals play in keeping us in a state of well-being. The atomic structures of nature, protons and electrons, form the basis of the elements, and these go on to form the enzymes and proteins that make up the body. In fact elements have some very interesting qualities and abilities, many of which test the known laws of physics.

For example, in the world of matter that surrounds us, gases can become liquids and liquids can become solids. The elements are in a dynamic state – continually building, repairing and changing. Gases become liquids with no prompting from us. It just happens as and when events and circumstance require it. For instance, as we have seen, two gas elements – hydrogen and oxygen – combine to form water, a liquid element which has some fascinating properties. Water makes up 65 per cent of our bodies; a common food such as the tomato is 95 per cent water and a chicken is saturated by 75 per cent water. In addition, almost 75 per cent of our planet is covered by it. On average, an adult contains about 38 litres of water and needs to replace 2 litres of that water every day. Without taking in water we would die within a few days.

Water is undoubtedly the most precious commodity for our

personal well-being and for the earth itself, but it behaves differently to many other liquids. Almost every other substance (whether solid, liquid or gas) shrinks as it cools; as its overall temperature decreases, it contracts and grows denser. But water behaves like other liquids until its temperature reaches 4 degrees centigrade; then something very strange happens. Water expands but gets lighter, and by the time its temperature reaches 0 degrees centigrade it has gained nearly 10 per cent in volume. This is why unprotected water pipes often burst in winter. More importantly, this property of water is essential to life on earth as we know it.

If water behaved like most other liquids it would sink instead of forming a protective, insulating layer over lakes and rivers. Vast sheets of ice would sink to the bottom of lakes and ponds, and the oceans of the world would solidify as the ice built up from the seabed. Life would certainly be very different.

The components of water – hydrogen and oxygen – are two of the most common elements. Hydrogen is number 1 on the table of elements and is the most abundant element in the universe, along with oxygen at number 8. Including other major elements, such as helium (number 2 on the table), carbon and phosphorus, there are a total of 103 elements that sustain us all every day of our lives. These elements, formed from the big bang, create our environment and fulfil all our nutritional needs.

This is what life is all about – the elements that feed our bodies and make the living matter around us. These elements appear to 'know' what to do without our conscious intervention. And all elements are actually composed of atoms.

As this book unfolds, you will come to understand that the electromagnetic forces that keep the atoms within the elements in our bodies functioning correctly are profoundly affected both positively and negatively, by the electromagnetic fields and energies of *thought*.

As I mentioned earlier, I find it difficult to imagine the concept of the earth being fifteen billion years old. Something else I find difficult to comprehend is the immense space existing between the infinitesimally small atoms that make up the elements of matter.

Dancing electrons

An atom in fact consists almost entirely of empty space, held together by electromagnetic forces and by the exchange of photons. In order to gain an understanding of this phenomenon, let's imagine that a typical atomic nucleus carrying a positive charge were the size of an aspirin. To get an idea of the distance between the nucleus (or aspirin) and the outer surrounding shell of electrons, imagine placing the aspirin at the centre of a football pitch in a stadium. The outer shell of the atom is the touchline (or where the crowd is seated). That's the enormity of the scale. Pure electricity (or is electromagnetic field) occupies the space between the centre nucleus and the outer shell. Just think of this immense distance or space that exists within matter. Not only do we comprise 65 per cent water, but the rest of our bodies are made up of empty space and dancing clouds of electrons. In reality, we are all hot air and water!

Everything that happens to us is actually electrical. No wonder we are so affected by the energies of our environment and the intensity of our thought processes. When you feel or touch 'something' you actually feel the interactions between the dancing electron clouds in the 'thing' you are touching and the dancing electron clouds on your fingertips. We have all experienced shocks caused by static electricity – perhaps when sliding across the seat of the car, when alighting and touching the door handle, or the hand of someone helping you from the car. Walk around a department store, particularly one with a nylon carpet, touch a lighted display cabinet with your hand, and it will give you a tingle every time. It's the electrons exchanging their minute charges that cause the tingle. So experience tells us we are all electric.

When messages about what we feel, touch, see, smell or taste are passed to our brains for assessment and action, they travel along networks of nerves by means of electrical impulses that stimulate chemical reactions. But all chemical reactions in the body simply consist of interactions between the electrons of the atoms existing within the body. When you read the words on this page, for example, light is absorbed into your eye, and you see by the interaction of light photons and electrons; yet inside your brain, where the words are perceived, there is absolute darkness.

When you listen to your favourite musical score, and respond perhaps to its emotional intensity, in your brain there is absolute silence. From the eardrum the resonance perceived is converted into electrical impulses that travel through the nervous system to the brain for interpretation. Likewise, when you respond to the aroma of your favourite dish and your taste buds are stimulated, or when you feel pain or heat or extreme cold, the sensation perceived is only electrical.

This is what we have to understand – that the body is not just a chemical or physical form made up of parts that we can actually see. There is so much more to the body – particularly those areas that we cannot see. It is in the minute, invisible spaces within the physical body, and in the electromagnetic fields of our thoughts, that the true causes of illness can take root and that true healing can take place.

The failings of the mechanistic model

The current mechanistic model of human beings used in conventional medicine is, I believe, outdated. The human body is not a machine. A typical machine, such as a motor car, contains parts that affects the performance of other parts. But, when all is said and done, one wheel cannot produce another wheel. The constituent parts of a machine exist *for* one another, not *because* of one another. In the case of the human body, the parts or cells have the ability to replicate, self-repair and self-reproduce. The life force that produces cells in the human body lies within the cells themselves. The body is a holistic entity – the cells affect the whole and the whole affects the cells.

In my opinion a major pitfall in orthodox medical procedures is that when you visit a conventional GP the diagnosis is only based upon the observable symptoms. The consultation consists of the patient describing the symptoms, drawing only upon their own feelings and interpretation of what ails them. For example, patients suffering headaches unsuccessfully treated by drugs or painkillers will be referred to a consultant in neurological matters for further advice or tests. These tests will be performed upon and about the head. No questions will be asked about diet, liver enzymes or the pancreas in which conditions may exist that could be causing the headaches. This mechanistic approach to medicine must change; we are not just a conglomeration of separate bits and pieces. Poor digestion affects the head, liver problems affect the skin, stress affects the adrenal glands, and so forth. The relationships are endless.

In future, medicine must take into account the manner in which nature has created and continues to create the human body in order to develop a more complete method of healing. It is in the unseen areas of creation, not in the chemical or biological domain, that we will find out the truth about the elemental make-up of the human form.

Breaking the code

As we have seen, the atoms that make up our cells, and their attendant fields of dancing electrons, are the very core of life. In addition we all have something called deoxyribonucleic acid (or DNA). This contains and transmits genetic information from cell to cell and is the key to our individuality. These elongated genetic codes are used in modern forensic science. For instance, the criminal who happens to sneeze during a robbery leaves a clue to his identity, because the structure of his genetic code is in every cell of his body, including his mucus membranes.

We are all made up of the same atoms and elements; yet we are all separate individuals. As well as having different fingerprints and genetic codes, we have differing characters and personalities; yet we are all made of the same physical matter derived from combinations of the 103 elements known to exist on this planet. These elements arrange themselves into complex compound structures to form life.

The whole world around us is formed from these 103 elements. For example, your dog and cat have organs within their bodies just like us. They have lungs, hearts and stomachs; they even have the same number of amino acids making up their DNA. They are made from elements and atoms – just like you and me.

So what makes some atoms and elements turn into animals and some into humans? Why do identical atomic structures go on to form some compounds that turn into frogs and others that turn into princes?

Scientists have concluded that continuing expansion since the big bang, fifteen billion years ago, has produced life on this planet that is governed by the atomic behaviour of the elements that make up the cells of our bodies. All living organisms are composed of different permutations and combinations of elements and the twenty-two amino acids. When these elements exist as individual elements and amino acids they have no biological properties – they are considered inorganic. But join them together to form proteins and they become the very essence of life. The fact that all living things share this life-generating core is thought-provoking, to say the least.

Could it possibly be that an as yet undiscovered elemental language, or essential vibrational cause, permeates the 103 elements and directs them to form the differing natural structures and species we see before us?

From little acorns . . .

In their unending search for answers, scientists have conducted extraordinary experiments, some of which have been designed to test the powers of nature and its ability to mend a wounded organism. However, nature always appears to strike back eventually, even if it takes time. For example, many plants will rise from the ashes of a forest fire renewed and invigorated.

Biological experiments on the poor frog cannot change it into a prince, but when a frog embryo is split in two at an early stage each half develops into a complete frog. Furthermore, if the part of the frog embryo that is destined to become an eye is similarly divided, the remainder goes on to form a complete eye (not just half an eye). This proves that within individual cells lies the pattern or blueprint of the whole structure – just as an acorn contains the blueprint of a giant oak.

The patterns and blueprints in the natural world remain intact, unseen, but potent for years and years. You can keep an acorn in a drawer for months or years, then plant it one season and watch it sprout. In the same way, nature keeps her secrets locked away for years and then one day surprises us. There are places on the dry scrubland of the north-western cape of South Africa which often amaze visitors with their panoramic vistas of multicoloured daisies. I have seen these majestic sites and wondered at their beauty, and I have encouraged others to return the next spring to see the spectacle, only to be told that when they arrived there was nothing but scrub and dry sand. Nature controls when seeds lie dormant and when they sprout, even when rain is plentiful.

Returning once more to the frog, if the whole eye structure is transplanted to the tail end of another frog embryo it does not grow into an eye on the tail but grows into a kidney or other organ appropriate to the area. Living tissue always behaves in a determined and assertive manner, restoring normality wherever possible. This is hard to explain in terms of Darwinian theory; it is not just a matter of chance but clearly a predetermined plan existing in the world of nature that creates men and mice from the same components.

Fruit flies are no exception to the rule. When scientists removed the genes that construct eyes they produced blind fruit flies. But they then found that, after the blind fruit flies had bred for a few generations, they somehow created eyes. The gene appeared all by itself, from nowhere; as always, nature fights back when we try to fool around with the order of the universe. The elements that make up the genes and organs of the body all work to a plan. Clearly, there is a structure to life; something is in control of the elements.

The language of the elements

Elements can exist on their own; or, as we have already mentioned, two of them can combine together to make water, for example. So why don't all the hydrogen elements (which predominate on the planet) grab all the lesser number of oxygen elements and form as much water as possible? Because it's all controlled. But by whom or what? Perhaps there really is a plan for life on earth, but who does it belong to? Certainly not the scientists, as their experiments to date should have taught them that nature will have its own way in the end. However, the lesson will probably not be learnt until much damage has been done to our environment. Only then will scientists finally learn that they cannot play God.

It also appears that the elements can communicate information from one part of the body to another by means of some unique universal language. This language or special system of communication can be understood by the nervous system (it is not just an electrical impulse that passes down a nerve fibre). It is understood as a vital need for cell survival and reproduction within the body.

Nutritional and metabolic needs are communicated from one cell to another and this can only be done by the atoms and electromagnetic fields that construct the elements and cells. I believe these electromagnetic fields can also interpret the energies of stress, love, hate, jealousy and greed. These emotions can be understood by the cells of the body, which make the necessary changes to adapt to the stresses that detrimentally affect the elemental structures of organs, glands and living tissue.

In medicine it is obvious that prolonged anxiety and worry will affect the performance of the human body by altering certain physical processes; eventually this will create diseased tissue and finally pathological illness. Long-term stress, for example, can create a peptic ulcer; worry can start an asthma attack.

Here lies a major clue. If we agree that thought processes can cause disease, then surely we must acknowledge that an undiscovered universal language permeates all living matter, from atoms to elements, and this language must be linked with thought processes.

A causal vibration of thought?

Thirty years of experience, and a database of information on patients' physical, mental and emotional problems, have shown me that fears, anxieties and stresses of many kinds, along with negative attitudes to life, are detrimental to our health; whereas positive thoughts, attitudes and aspirations are essential for our health. Could it be that all living matter on earth has a causal vibration of thought that emanates from the very elements that make up the earth? Do the known elements of the earth actually have a language and a mind of their own?

When Francis Crick was unravelling the mysteries of the double helix of DNA in the 1950s he questioned why a wounded organism should recreate its structure and functions exactly as they had existed before it was damaged. The fact is that the information needed to achieve this must already exist within our bodies. The codes locked up in the chromosomes of all living organisms have the same chemical substance and use the same code script, which implies that the genetic information contained in one cell must be identical to that in all cells. So how on earth can cells specialise? How do they know when to repair, when to coagulate blood, and when to send immune cells to the site of a wound?

How do the billions of cells that all magically evolved from one fertilised egg, that at its conception had no specialised qualities, mystically know how to create the human form and become muscle cells or blood cells and so on?

Questions such as these help to explain why there is now a groundswell of opinion among many biologists, scientists and doctors that molecular biology has reached its limits. The intelligence that directs and shapes elemental matter into organic living forms remains profoundly mysterious – the possible existence of an elemental yet silent language of thought processes within and around the structures of our bodies has to be considered. And this raises the question: are there thoughts that can harm our minds and bodies, and likewise thoughts that can heal? Is there actually order within the atoms and elements that make up our bodies? And does this help to explain why some chronically ill patients die, while others displaying chronic symptoms survive to enjoy a long, healthy life?

The nature of the human form is very hard to fathom. The more I enquire, the more imponderables I find. Even scientists, in their ceaseless quest to prove or disprove what they see in the world of nature, find ever more mysteries in the course of their experiments. This totally confounds their understanding of the man-made laws they have created for chemistry, biology and physics.

For years I have pondered why some patients survive and others die, as science already admits that the cells of the body actually know how to replicate, repair and self-reproduce a total human being. If perfection existed in all structures, illness in the human organism could last no longer than approximately six months, the time it takes for certain cells to replicate in the body. There are still many unexplained mind–body phenomena – maybe the answer lies in karma, fate or destiny? Call it what you like, there seems to be some overriding force that finally decides whether we recover or remain ill.

Chemotherapy will cure some patients, yet kill others. Complementary medicine and many of the alternative therapies suffer similar inconsistencies. I believe that medical science is barking up the wrong tree by only focusing on chemistry and biology when it comes to understanding the cause of illness. I think the answers exist in the pages of books on quantum physics and on various alternative therapies. Unanimity actually does exist between all branches of medicine but on just one point – that the core of life exists within the atomic structures of the human body.

Order and disorder

A physicist by the name of Schrodinger explained that the probable lifetime of a single atom is much less certain than that of a healthy sparrow. Indeed, nothing more can be said about it than this: As long as the atom exists, the chances of it disappearing into thin air are the same as that of the sparrow dying in the next second; the probabilities for both remain exactly the same. In other words, you cannot predict anything with certainty.

The future behaviour of any individual atom and its clouds of electrons, within any element that forms part of a cell or organ, has no relation to its past history or actions; yet there is an overall pattern to its existence. Science has established the patterns and time schedules of decay in atoms – this is known as radioactivity. Physics states that the disintegration of any single atom is totally unpredictable, yet the behaviour of large numbers of such atoms is assured.

So, if disorder becomes widespread in an organism, the outcome will be orderly, based upon the behaviour of the original patterns of disorder. This is why, when a body begins a self-destruct path (as in an auto-immune disease), it destroys itself in an orderly fashion, thinking it is the right thing to do. In other cases the disease patterns within the elements often correct themselves, based upon the number of healthy cells remaining in the organism. The same phenomenon (of the largest number of atoms dictating the pattern of behaviour) assures order within the organism.

This process can be assisted by positive, correct thoughts that will cause the healthy cells to replicate rather than the rogue cells. And this is why some people get well and others die. It depends whether stable atoms in the healthy cells or unstable atoms in the rogue cells predominate in the area of the body affected by the illness.

The stability of atoms relies solely upon the constancy of their own electromagnetic fields. Electrical interference will disturb the order within the atomic structure, and disorder and illness will be the result. This is why it is important to conduct research into the effects of cellular phones and microwave energy on the brain cells.

If a physician can establish the cause for a set of symptoms and then provide an environment within the patient that will create sufficient numbers of atoms of order, then healing will result. True healing can only occur if the elemental particles in the body are in balance. No amount of chemotherapy or invasive therapy will heal if the elementary cause is unknown.

The most important influence upon the elementary particles is electrical interference, and the most common and most powerful type of electrical interference is *thought*.

Chapter Four

THE POWER OF THOUGHT

I SCAN THE SHOPPING list Chrissie gave me before leaving home; I seem to have bought everything needed and make my way to the checkout. Standing there, I suddenly think I ought to get an extra loaf of bread, although I will lose my place in the queue. However, I wander off to the bakery department, add more weight to my basket and join the back of the now longer queue for the checkout. As I arrive home, Chrissie greets me with the news that the family are coming for afternoon tea and she is worried that we are short of bread.

Did I pick up the thought that Louise and Kevin had telephoned half an hour earlier? Or was it Chrissie thinking that we didn't have enough bread for sandwiches? And why did I suddenly decide to go back to the bakery when I had bought everything on the list? Where did the thought about the need for extra bread come from?

I am sure all of you reading this have experienced similar events, when a thought suddenly comes to mind for no apparent reason and then, some time later, an event will occur that explains why the thought arose. So where do thoughts come from, where do they reside and how do we pick them up and act upon them?

Mind over matter

The power contained within a thought, and its effect upon the human body in connection with both well-being and illness, has largely been ignored by conventional medicine, apart from that segment dealing with psychiatry. However, many complementary practitioners employ the term 'mind–body medicine' and consider that thought plays an important role both in the causes of illness and in the subsequent healing process.

In my own traditional naturopathic practice I use various well-proven diagnostic techniques in conjunction with a computer assessment program developed from my database of nearly 4000 patient case histories. The accumulation of data and the subsequent development of a diagnostic program have successfully shown that thought, attitudes, stresses and anxieties can be major factors in causing ill-health, and by correcting these disruptive elements, well-being can be attained. I often tell my patients to keep their goals and aspirations in their minds at all times – take your eye off the finishing post and the hurdles get in the way.

Doctors trained in classical homeopathy, as I have been, take time to observe patients during a consultation; it's not just the questions they ask, it's how the patients answer, and the mannerisms they display. Each of my patients completes a questionnaire. When compared to my database of symptoms and related attitudes and aspirations, this sheds considerable light on the cause of their own personal symptoms.

For example, the heart, circulation, vagus nerve and immune system all respond to positive thoughts of calmness, love of humanity, patience and understanding. The opposite of these thoughts (coldness and indifference to others, selfishness and fear) will bring about disease symptoms. Narrow-mindedness, clumsy attitudes and lack of sympathy will adversely affect both the male and female reproductive systems, whereas accuracy and a strong sense of justice with original ideas will heal symptoms of the generative organs.

I have categorised many attitudes over the years, linked to various illnesses, and found that, by instilling reverence for life, caring attitudes to others, and respect for relationships, patients with digestive disorders got better. I also found that twelve basic elements, such as potassium, magnesium, calcium and other minerals, were closely related to certain attitudes.

This way of thinking was nothing new, as doctors in the past categorised physical, mental and emotional symptoms with the use of biochemic tissue salts and elements. However, in my experience, the natural remedies improved patients' positive attitudes, which indicated the links between thinking processes and the elements of the earth and what we feed upon as humans. Furthermore, I suggested to patients that they needed aspirations in life and that they should visualise their desires.

To do this, it is very important to see in your mind's eye that which you wish to accomplish – in your career, your general day-to-day existence and your personal relationships. Thus, when illness strikes you should visualise yourself enjoying renewed health; do not put any energy into worrying about how you will fulfil the goal of well-being, as the action of correct thinking will enable you to overcome the obstacles as long as you are focussed on the positive aspiration. It really is a case of 'mind over matter'.

Positive and negative thinking

Thought is clearly the greatest creative force within the universe, as it precedes all our actions – both physical and mental. No event happens in our lives and no material object is created on this planet that did not originate as a thought. Thought precedes everything and is the most powerful medium for transferring energy. Put your energies into positive ideas and aspirations and watch them manifest. The very act of thinking has a major influence on the body every second of every day of our lives. It can cause changes in blood supply, blood pressure and pulse rate.

For example, after a long period of mental concentration, the body will become tired and sluggish, making it more difficult to concentrate and complete a task. Thought can be a constructive agent, but it can also be destructive in relation to our well-being. Good health is obviously more enjoyable than ill-health; even so, there are those who seem to enjoy the latter. Some patients actually appear to derive pleasure from the attention they gain from being ill. Even though the illness causes them stress, they make little effort to gain an improvement in their symptoms. Many different terms are used to express the power of thought in relation to illness – psychosomatic, self-limiting, hysterical, and so on.

Sarah's was a case in point – where thoughts of unnecessary guilt had caused very serious physical symptoms to develop. Five and a half years before she came to my clinic, Sarah had been involved in a tragic accident where a girl, the same age as her own daughter, accidentally lost her life. Sarah had been cleared of any blame but, because of her overcaring nature, became totally distraught about the incident. She had suffered a nervous breakdown and then went on to develop skin symptoms, circulation problems, digestive disorders and difficulties with lymphatic drainage.

It took many consultations to make Sarah change her thoughts and attitude to the unfortunate affair. It required a reversal of her guilt feelings and a shedding of her remorse. I had to instil into Sarah that she still had good reasons to go on living, even though – at that time – she saw none at all.

I created an optimum potential report for Sarah and showed her all the wonderful attributes and qualities she possessed. I pointed out her caring, loving nature, her powerful intuition and perception, and – most of all – her deep understanding of the needs of others. I indicated that her continuing worry and stress about the accident had caused her logical brain to disregard the all-important fact that no blame had been apportioned to her.

'Let the right and left brain hemispheres work together' was one of my suggestions. I advised her to embark upon some creative hobby or work that would stimulate both sides of her brain, as she was thinking negatively through the left side only. This was the cause of her continuing depression and her stomach symptoms. As the digestion was the seat of her emotions, the shock of the event had put her stomach into a total spin. I also talked to Sarah about the skin being an organ that rids itself of unwanted toxins. The continual guilt was an unwanted burden and, as an energetic force, was exiting through her skin in the form of lesions and sebaceous cysts.

Sarah and I had many long talks in order to reinstall, so to speak, her wonderful attributes and abilities into her conscious mind (which had been totally deprogrammed by the tragic event). I gave Sarah some Dr Bach flower essences, along with homeopathic remedies and vitamin supplements which began to clear the physical symptoms. Best of all, Sarah has returned to being herself – caring, humorous, intuitive, perceptive, and enjoying life to the full.

Feeling the fear

Thoughts can affect the body in so many ways, but probably the most powerful aspect of thought, and the major cause of illness in our Western civilisation, is fear. This emotion can weaken the constitution and compromise the immune system. Fear produces panic about the future of one's health and well-being. Patients come to me saying they have just received a bombshell: the doctor has told them it's cancer, and nothing can be done. The impersonal way in which these 'men in white coats' deliver judgement on a patient's life is wholly inappropriate.

The anxiety, panic, fear, shock and trauma experienced at the time of diagnosis is probably more detrimental to the patient than the damage being wreaked upon his or her body by the cancer. Cancer cells are not as strong as people believe; it is the support cancer cells receive from negative thinking that allows them to proliferate. As we have seen, atoms and their dancing clouds of electrons will be affected by a predominance of either order or disorder within the body; and, in the midst of severe despondency and despair at receiving such news, negative disorder will proliferate and the illness will get worse. Radical changes must take place in the patient's thought processes in order to restore order within the atoms forming the physical body.

Pat's was another case that proved beyond a shadow of doubt the power thought exercised over the physical body. A friend brought Pat to me in April 1995, as she was unable to drive herself at the time, being rather weak after undergoing a recent operation on her oesophagus and further cancer treatments. Pat had actually had cancer thirty years before I saw her, and had endured a radical mastectomy, radiation and then – unbelievably – a spleenectomy in error. Can you imagine enduring such a catalogue of events and still being told the prognosis was unfavourable? When I took the case history from Pat I saw that she was a woman with courage second to none.

I started Pat on a regime consisting of large doses of mineral ascorbates to support her immune system. This enhanced the natural cancer cell killer activity by helping the white blood cells move to the site where they were needed. This type of vitamin C is essential for the production of collagen and connective tissue. (Remember Pat had no spleen for her own immunity and her connective tissue had been impaired by previous radio-therapy.) Elemental celloids were also prescribed, along with appropriate homeopathic remedies and some further supplements of echinacea and hydrastis.

However, the primary mode of treatment was the use of Pat's powerful mind energies, so I had to determine why the cancer had started way back in 1967. This took a few visits in which we discussed Pat's childhood, and then the events in her life, right up to the last ten years when all the problems manifested again. The saga was unbelievable: Pat had suffered abuse – both physical and mental – at the hands of a family member, and had lost her mother when she was very young. She had been forcibly taken from her home at the age of nine and had been plagued all her life by feelings of insecurity and the fear of offending others. Yet, underneath all this, she was a loving and caring person. From the age of nine Pat had been raised in an Irish convent, totally devoid of family relationships. She even spent Christmases alone when all the other children went home. When Pat was eighteen her father suddenly contacted her and she was taken to England. These years of loneliness and abuse had subdued Pat's own personality and the innate qualities she possessed.

I entered Pat's details into my computer and found that underlying all this debris which cluttered her personality, was a core of inner truth, overcaring for others, wisdom and understanding, along with perception and innate intuition. I spoke at length to Pat about these attributes which she felt had been suppressed by the strong convictions of other people for so long that she had forgotten how she used to be. We met and talked each month and slowly she began to realise that, by standing back from her existing health situation and the restrictions it placed on her life, she could see herself as she really was before the years of abuse.

Now Pat was able to see the beauty in the world around her. She watched the birds in the garden, saw the wonder in the flowers, invited more visitors to her house, became more open and, best of all, gained the confidence to start driving again. After five years of regular consultations and a regime of maintenance supplements, Pat remains well and has amazed her orthodox physicians who, back in 1995, gave her but a few months to live.

This was a case of establishing the cause of the initial cancer, then drawing on the innate character of the patient and the thoughts associated with her attributes and using them to prevent the formation of rogue cells in the body. Pat was able to keep the cancer cells in a controlled and isolated environment within her body and this is a task for which the immune system is specifically designed. At present, with the correct attitudes and thoughts uppermost in her mind, any rogue cancer cells that dare raise their heads above the parapet are speedily annihilated by the stronger and more dominant immune cells. I firmly believe the body can isolate and imprison a tumour in such a manner, whilst the patient enjoys a comparatively normal state of well-being.

'Ghostly action'

In order to understand how this can happen, we have to establish how and where thoughts arise and the procedure the mind uses in healing. How do thoughts travel, where do they come from, and where do they go when dealt with? Do they reside inside or outside the brain? Do they exist in the past or present? And are there thoughts out there, waiting for us to perceive them tomorrow? It's all a bit of a mystery; but, once again, the study of quantum physics sheds some light on the workings of thought.

Albert Einstein believed that no signal or influence could travel faster than the speed of light. He dismissed the idea of electrons influencing each other's motion and position – even a few metres apart, let alone light years apart. Unfortunately his theory was flawed, as proved by a complex experiment conducted many years ago. It was carried out by three eminent physicists, one of whom was Einstein himself, and demonstrated that two electrons separated by light years in distance could influence each other's actions. In fact the mere action of thinking about making changes to the properties of one electron was found to affect the other electron light years away instantaneously. (Giant particle accelerators enable physicists to simulate distances as large as light years using quantum principles.) The EPR experiment – so-called after the eminent physicists Einstein, Podolsky and Rosen – drew attention to this phenomenon as far back as the 1930s.

The experiment involves two balanced spinning electrons; both share the same axis but are spinning in different directions. They are then separated from one another by a huge distance (let's say particle 1 is in New York and particle 2 is in Los Angeles or on the other side of the world). Yet this enormous separation does not interfere with their spin or axis. The crucial point about the experiment is that the instant an observer of particle 1 makes a measurement or change of spin or axis, particle 2 changes its axis or spin accordingly.

There is no time for particle 2 to receive information about the change by any conventional signal. A measurement performed on one particle has an instant effect on the other far distant particle. Einstein called this 'ghostly action at a distance'.

In the face of this, the theory of relativity (based on the premise that nothing travels faster than the speed of light) collapses. The 'action at a distance' experiment proves that thought and the energies preceding thought (that is, thinking about taking action) can travel faster than the speed of light. In fact, thought is instantaneous. Thought can affect the actions of electrons, which in turn affect the performance of the atoms they govern, which then affect the performance of the elements which make up all living matter. This is how positive or negative thought can bring about well-being or ill-health. It is very important for people to realise, however, that exterior negative thoughts can only be received if the recipient is open to them.

The voodoo man must get your attention before casting his spell – whether it is through a symbol on the door or just making his presence known.

In Cape Town, many years ago, I knew an office clerk whose father was a witchdoctor. He explained that even the most powerful of medicine men had to make their patients aware of their intent. I remember walking down the street and asking my African friend if the knowledge handed down to him by his father could influence a passer-by on the other side of the street. He said it could not, unless he presented that person with a symbol of intent. Then he would have them under his power! This illustrates again the powerful effect of fear.

The secret life of plants

The power of thought exists in the world of nature in general (not only amongst humans). I was very fortunate to lecture on the same platform, back in the early eighties, with Christopher Bird, a world-renowned biologist and anthropologist. A few years earlier Christopher had joined forces with Peter Tompkins and together they wrote a book called *The Secret Life of Plants*. This exciting book catalogues some extraordinary experiments that showed how plants bent towards the music of Beethoven and Bach, for example, but recoiled from rock and roll.

The most interesting experiment involved tomato plants which were hooked up to a type of ECG instrument that registered electrical impulses and the changes in electrical activity of the cell structures in the plants. The plants were left in the laboratory for some time, and the electrical activity they generated was at a mean or average level. People would enter the room, take readings of the graphs and make general observations.

After a period of time, when equilibrium was well-established in the laboratory and people were entering and leaving the room daily, a technician was sent in and he set about burning the leaves of some of the plants with a lighted match. Naturally the burnt plants registered excessive electrical activity and disturbance on the graph. But, interestingly, so did those plants he did not burn. The laboratory was then left to have equilibrium restored; other technicians who had previously completed readings on charts entered and left the room, and the leaves of the burnt plants began to heal.

Some considerable time elapsed before the technician who had previously burnt the plants entered the room. He had no lighted match in his hand, he just appeared at the door; but all the plants registered sudden electrical activity on the recording graphs. They seemed to recognise or perceive the culprit even after many days' absence. Was it thought, was it just innate perception? Whatever it was, some form of intelligent response emanated from those tomato plants that was recorded as electrical impulses.

The myth of objective perception

In human medicine organic disease is often attributed to factors such as a weakened immune system. However the immune system was probably weakened by inadequate nourishment, which was in turn caused by the patient feeling stressed. As usual, the thought comes before the reaction in the body.

As well as influencing our physical reactions, our thoughts affect our perception of what goes on around us. This can be particularly problematic when it comes to so-called objective laboratory results for blood tests and smear tests. To understand the problems that can occur, we need to consider some rather complex questions about how we perceive reality.

Let's say you are walking alongside a railway line at a steady pace. You have just passed a farmer leaning on a fence beside the railway track when you see a train approaching. The speed of the train is 50 miles an hour. As it passes you, going in the opposite direction to the way you are walking, you see a person walking down the central corridor on the train. The person on the train is walking in the opposite direction to which the train is moving but in the same direction as you. At what speed would you say the person on the train was walking, given that walking speed is approximately 4 miles an hour?

Your first reaction is probably to start adding or subtracting 4 miles from 50, then perhaps adding another 4 and so forth. But in fact the person walking down the central corridor on the train is walking at many different speeds all at the same time. It just depends where the observer is looking from. Or, as Einstein might have said, it's all relative.

To the farmer leaning on the fence, the train walker's speed is 46 miles an hour. To other people sitting on the train it is 4 miles an hour; and to you, the walker beside the track, it is 42 miles an hour. Yet the train itself is travelling at 50 miles an hour. The train walker is also travelling in different directions at the same time. It all depends where the observation or measurement is taken from. So the bizarre reality is that the train walker is able to move in two directions at the same time and at differing speeds. You can choose any of the answers – they are all correct.

Another distorting factor is the way we interpret statistics. Think of two newly minted coins, indistinguishable from one another, but of the same value. If you toss the coins you might see three different outcomes. There may be two heads showing uppermost, or two tails, or one of each. So you may initially consider that you have a one-in-three chance of getting a head–tail combination, or all heads or all tails. But a little thought shows that this is not the case. Suppose you marked one of the coins in some way, so that the two coins are now distinguishable from one another. Now you can see that, although there is only one way to get the combination head–head and one way to get tail–tail, there are two ways of getting the head–tail combination: one is head–tail, the other is tail–head. Either coin can be 'head', provided the other one comes up tails. So the correct way to interpret the outcome is one-in-four and not one-in-three as you initially thought.

Thinking ourselves ill

Combine the unreliable interpretation of statistics (the coin experiment) with the relative viewpoint of the observer (the train walker), and the instantaneous influence of one electron on another far distant one (the EPR experiment), and we start to understand why, in any test, experiment or research, the thoughts of the operator or observer have a major influence on the final outcome and result.

Medical science has made major advances in the assessment and diagnostic procedures used in the fight against cancer, and women are now urged to have regular breast scans and cervical smears. This is highly commendable and has made the early detection of cancer possible. The taking of cervical cells from women, and the testing for pre-cancerous cells, has two basic flaws in my opinion. Firstly, cells taken from the body are no longer under the influence of the patient's immune system. The atomic structures within the removed cells will therefore behave differently from the way they behave in the patient's body. Secondly, the systems and procedures used in laboratories differ, and the technicians themselves – although trained in obtaining medical data – will be unaware of the way they influence the results. (The EPR experiment proves this.) If an observer expects to find cancer cells in a smear test there is more chance that they will. The observer can completely change the outcome of the smear test, because the observer's electromagnetic fields influence the electromagnetic fields of the cells being tested. (In view of these problems it is scarcely strange that there have been so many inaccurate smear test results. The only surprise is that conventional medicine has given the smear test procedure such credence.)

Furthermore, the sample of tissue or blood taken from the donor patient is no longer under the influence of the donor's own electromagnetic fields of force and dancing electron clouds. The influence now, in terms of electron activity, is purely from the observer of the test equipment designed to find cancer cells.

The process of a patient being called back for a further smear test is in itself detrimental. The thoughts of fear and panic aroused by the prospect of a second test will encourage disorderly cells to proliferate in a suddenly changed environment of despondency and despair within the body. This will result in a differing set of readings from the first set, causing even more consternation.

As we have seen, one disorderly atom, particle or cell can influence other cells to believe that disorder is desirable. This leads to a self-destructive chain reaction and is likely to prove conclusive. In this sense, blood and tissue tests can sometimes be more of a hindrance than a help.

I see many patients whose tests prove negative but they feel unwell; while others go for routine tests feeling well physically but apprehensive mentally and a few weeks later they are given a terminal diagnosis.

Women suffer far more than men when it comes to regular testing for cancer. Although men over the age of fifty are now advised to have tests for prostate cancer, women are still the main focus of attention. Significantly, most of the surgery carried out on women is conducted by men. I wonder if the same number of tests and surgical procedures would be carried out if there were more women doctors treating male patients?

This is not to say that testing is always harmful. It can sometimes lead to early detection and successful treatment of disease.

However, the testing procedure (and communication of results) needs to be carried out with great tact and sensitivity so that the benefits outweigh the anxiety caused. Thoughts are so powerful and influential that the media, particularly advertising, can cause all manner of negative emotional feelings to manifest within us. These insidious thoughts linger and then produce physical symptoms, often due to inner worry and anxiety – created to swell the coffers of healthcare companies. For instance, there are TV adverts showing a female motorist stranded in her car on a rain-soaked motorway; the overhead road signs start flashing her name, telling her she feels unwell and needs to have a free medical with a major healthcare consortium. We have drug companies sponsoring weather bulletins that include reports of pollen counts up and down the country, advising sufferers to 'be ready; go and get your prescription even if you have sneezed only once today; tomorrow's going to be bad for hayfever sufferers'.

These are the sorts of negative thoughts that constantly bombard us through the media. They are often wrapped up in an agreeable, humorous form, yet the hidden agenda is always to induce anxiety in order to make us do certain things and buy certain products. Promotions and publicity agencies know only too well how powerful thought can be.

Thought and memory

From your earliest days in the womb (when your mother's thoughts affected you) to the thoughts you are having while reading this book, every thought you've ever had has travelled through your biological systems and most have activated a physiological response. In an adult that amounts to countless millions of thoughts, causing just as many chemical reactions. A thought of fear, for instance, will activate your fight and flight mechanism:

some people experience prickling sensations under their arms, or a strange taste on the tongue, their heart rate may increase and they probably break out in a sweat. A loving thought, on the other hand, will relax you, inducing a sense of calm throughout your physical body.

Thoughts, regardless of their content, enter your body as an energetic field of force and react to the dancing clouds of electron around the atoms within the cells. Some pass through your systems without causing any noticeable effect; others are perceived as requiring attention and cause you to act immediately.

Many thoughts are stored in our memories: thoughts of known or unknown fears – feelings of dread about the future. These stored thoughts are often the result of traumatic mental and emotional or even physical experiences.

For instance, in the great storm that struck the southern counties of England in the late eighties, a patient of mine witnessed large pine trees falling around her property and was fearful for her own safety. During a respite in the wind she left the house to go to a friend whose garden had fewer trees. But while she was walking the short distance to her neighbour's there was a huge gust of wind and a large oak fell right on top of her. Miraculously, as she stood frozen with fear, the falling tree deposited one large branch to her left and another to her right. She emerged totally unscathed physically. However, the mental scars remain. Whenever the wind whistles past her house or she sees the trees swaying in a gentle breeze, the fear and panic well up within her. Her heart races, her blood sugar levels change and she feels an adrenaline surge as she relives the fear she experienced that day many years ago.

Other thoughts that patients secrete away are those of inferiority complexes and obsessions – all these attitudes of mind, sometimes triggered by a physical phenomenon or event, are held in the memory.

A pattern emerges

It was my overwhelming interest in the way patients responded to the thoughts I implanted in their minds as part of my treatment that made me start gathering information for my database. I wanted to find out which thoughts affected which part of the body and what types of symptoms were regularly displayed. I began to correlate the patient data in various categories: general area of the body affected with type of symptom; known mineral deficiencies with area of the body and symptoms; attitudes and anxieties prior to experiencing symptoms; mineral and vitamin supplements successfully used for areas of the body and known symptoms; corrected thoughts and attitudes given with supplements that effected a cure; and corrected thoughts and attitudes that effected a cure on their own.

I ended up with a paper mountain but I knew I was on to something, as a pattern started to emerge that enabled me to link attitudes with illness and identify which areas of the body were affected by certain types of symptoms. Likewise, attitudes and thoughts to effect cures also emerged. Gradually patients began making recoveries from chronic illness, using a combination of elemental minerals and specialised dietary supplements, but particularly the sets of thoughts and attitudes that I would type out for each person (as each individual required different attitudes in order to manage their illness).

To my delight, one of my long-standing patients, Maureen Bartlett, became aware of the system, showed tremendous interest and realised its potential, not only for patients but for practitioners who could use the information for the benefit of all patients, whether they were practising conventional or alternative medicine. The computer disc of this system is soon to be made available to the medical profession.

Now, thanks to our good friend Maureen, the paper mountain that Chrissie and I created over many years is safely installed in a computer program. When Maureen saw the results of our research she insisted that it should be computerised so that we could access the information quickly and easily. The result of her generosity is a computer program that allows individual reports to be produced for individual patients no matter what the illness or treatment protocol.

The program first establishes the strengths of the patient's constitution and character, which is a great help in understanding why people subjected to similar stressful environments or the same bacteria and viruses will not all develop similar illnesses or symptoms. Our research has established what types of people will suffer what types of illnesses, based upon their individual physical constitutions and personality characteristics. This is vitally important for all branches of medicine: understanding the inner strengths of the patient suffering a particular type of illness enables the practitioner to target the treatment far more accurately. He or she can deal specifically with the weakest areas of the general constitution, irrespective of the symptoms.

Once the patient develops a sense of general well-being, healing slowly follows. Add to this the correct healing attitudes and thoughts and the regenerative abilities of the body's cells are heightened. Our research has shown emphatically that people suffering continual anxiety about their own health, overcaring for those close to them emotionally, and suffering fear of unknown future events, were predisposed to immune deficiency illnesses. Those people who coped more easily with emotional upsets, who had a more accepting attitude and 'just got on with life', had strong immune systems and circulation.

People who had thoughts of uncertainty and could not decide between one thing and another, were full of hopelessness and self-doubt, along with lack of ambition, suffered from skeletal conditions and backache with kidney symptoms. Those who took no real interest in life and just sailed along in their own little world, continually thinking about the past instead of looking to the future, had stomach problems. Those who found little joy in life, had gloomy moods, and did not learn from previous mistakes, appeared to suffer lower bowel conditions.

Oversensitive people with inner jealousies and those with suspicious natures had generative organ symptoms; lonely and non-communicative people suffered respiratory illness, along with thyroid conditions. Despondent yet hard-working people suffered left-sided headaches; those with fixed principles and unbending attitudes had right-sided headaches. And so the research unfolded – to produce a complete program of thoughts and attitudes that were harmful and created symptoms of illness, and thoughts and attitudes that were healing. The result of all these years of research is the A–Z in Part Two of this book.

Chapter Five

MORE THOUGHTS ABOUT THOUGHT

T HE SEARING HEAT of the African sun scorched the cab of my four-wheel drive as I sat with both doors fully open, allowing the hot draught to vaporise the beads of sweat on my face. As the BBC World Service crackled quietly from beneath the dashboard, I was suddenly aware of penetrating eyes. I was being observed by a small band of bushmen who, like me, had been surveying a waterhole from a safe distance. Slowly they approached and a pidgin English conversation ensued. The bony, leathery-skinned bushmen questioned me with astonishment about the voices coming from inside the cab, yet they saw me sitting alone. Explanations about radio waves, or a voice travelling through the air from London to the African veld, amazed them. They peered beneath the dashboard at my invitation, bemused by what they heard.

Suddenly their interest shifted; they began a tongue-clicking chatter and informed me that another band of bushmen many miles to the east (one of whom was the elder's brother), had made a kill and they would all eat supper that evening. 'How do you know that?' I asked in my mixture of pidgin English and Afrikaans. 'He say it in here,' said the elder, pointing to his head, and off they loped.

So, who had the best means of communication, me with my twentieth-century radio listening to the World Service or the bushman picking up thoughts from his brother all those miles away? This was one of my first experiences of thought transference, used instinctively and accepted as completely natural by a people so unaffected by the stress of modern life that thinking was, in their eyes, an intrinsic part of communication.

The memory of cells

Vast resources have been consumed in the endless quest to understand the workings of the human brain, but our knowledge is still very limited. Little is known about whether or where thoughts are stored in the brain. We really don't know where the memory is situated. We know that the two hemispheres of the brain are linked by a major nerve ganglion, acting as a bridge between our creative (right-sided) brain and our logical (left-sided) brain. But science is confounded by the fact that large parts of the brain can be removed without destroying memory.

There is also the fact that certain cells of the brain behave in a similar manner to others in the body in terms of reproducing themselves, while others die off completely. Take this another step forward and examine the physical body in general. The cells of your body are in a continual dynamic state of reproduction and replication – not one cell remains in your body today that was evident a few years ago. Yet cells do appear to possess some form of memory, as I can personally testify.

More than twenty-five years ago I severely damaged my left knuckle. The wound was inflicted by a glancing blow with a large and lethal hammer in the hands of a short-sighted person. The blow took the skin and soft tissue away and exposed the knucklebone. It took a long time to heal, even with the use of large amounts of vitamin E and bathing in pure seawater. I had a patient at the time who worked on the deep-sea trawlers that sailed out of Cape Town. I asked him to collect for me a few gallons of unpolluted seawater from the far reaches of the South Atlantic and I would soak my hand in a small amount for a quarter of an hour every day. Eventually it healed and now shows no signs of a scar or blemish.

My memory of the event is clear, but the cells of the skin, tissue and the bone are renewed and no physical trauma can possibly exist in the area today. The brain cells that registered the pain and the event have also long gone. But every time I pick up a hammer, or find myself near someone who is about to hammer a nail or suchlike, the knuckles on my left hand begin to tingle. Does this mean that memory exists outside the brain? Are thoughts transferred from cell to cell, as an energetic field holding the memory of all the events that have happened in our lives?

The emotions of cells

Perhaps thought is stored in every cell of the body – maybe each one contains the whole blueprint of a person's life, along with the genetic information from our forebears. I must admit, as I get older, I do look and think more and more like my father. We all contain genetic material from our parents, yet we are all unique individuals with unique DNA codes. As we know, the whole body recreates itself every six months by renewing all the cells that make up the physical structure. But, as illness often lasts longer than six months, our memories and thoughts must surely be transferred in the metabolic processes of our cells. However, because we cannot measure thoughts of love, of hate, jealousy, pride and other emotions, we cannot prove their existence in our cells.

Orthodox medicine does acknowledge that an 'endergonic process' (defined in the medical dictionary as 'the *absorption* of energy along with the input of *free* energy') occurs within cells.

This indicates an understanding of a subtle but unknown source of energy that affects the actions of cells and body structures, which could of course include thought, as this is energetic in its nature.

The emotional energies stored in cells have been dramatically demonstrated in some of the cases I have treated. For instance, I knew a lawyer who developed asthma because he defended a case where he knew the client was not disclosing the full facts and he felt his own moral integrity was being undermined. This undisclosed information was perceived by his subconscious mind, and the energies released caused an illness to develop in the area of communication. He could not consciously accept the wrongdoing, so the emotional energy of articulation – being totally blocked – turned the energy inwards and caused an asthma attack. These attacks continued until the patient openly discussed his inner fears and anxieties, and as the emotional energy reduced in intensity so did the asthma.

One small event can affect a single cell, which can then multiply to cause a pathological condition or illness. This was the case with a financial consultant who developed a very painful spot on his neck. It progressed to form a larger and more pronounced skin lesion, which went on to become a rash that mimicked eczema. No ointment or cream could calm the redness and irritation and the man became very embarrassed by his appearance. After approximately six months he came to see me and we discussed his work in some detail. I tried to persuade him to tell me if he was hiding something that was causing him inner stress. Eventually, after the third visit, he admitted that he was covering up for the inadequacies of a colleague at work. The stress was affecting his digestion and his liver in particular and he had been suffering from long-term constipation.

I told him to speak to the colleague, who was probably unaware of the problem. I also asked my patient if the situation could be rectified – was his friend up to making the changes required?

He felt that a conclusion to benefit all parties could be reached, but he himself was very sensitive to the needs of others and disliked the thought of any acrimony arising between himself and the colleague. We therefore discussed a strategy based upon the strengths of my patient's character.

He would approach the man in a friendly manner, explaining that a helping hand was being offered to him. He would suggest that maybe if the colleague changed tack, worked a little differently, did some home study and took a little work home it would hasten his chances of promotion. It worked, the situation improved, and in four weeks the skin rash was gone. From this simple example we can see how the emotions generated by a small event can affect a few cells that then multiply to affect thousands.

'Thoughtstrings'

Modern cloning techniques suggest that the genetic material for the whole body exists in a single cell. Likewise, perhaps the whole of a person's thinking exists in a single cell (of which there are billions in the adult human body). We accept that the mind and body are intrinsically linked when it comes to attaining well-being, and medicine considers that thoughts and the mind exist within the brain. However, perhaps we need to step beyond familiar boundaries and consider the possibility that the mind is *outside* the brain. The mind of the whole person appears to exist in every cell, which itself contains the structures of the elements that make up the physical body. It is in these electromagnetic fields that the ability to continually receive and project thoughts seems to lie. And, as we know, researchers have proved that parts of the brain can be surgically removed without destroying memory of past events; therefore memory is not solely biological or chemical.

In their search for a theory to explain everything that exists in the universe, physicists have come up with the idea of superstrings. They suggest that the building blocks of the universe – that is the protons, neutrons and electrons – are not elementary particles, as had long been assumed, but rather tiny massless strings that vibrate at a specific frequency and twist and rotate in space. In other words they are a form of energy without visible mass that surrounds and yet is part of the elemental material that makes up our planet. Absurd as it may sound, the superstring theory promises to provide a unified description of all the forces of nature and the particles of matter, including that of the human body. This theory is also founded upon elegant mathematical ideas that prove consistent with the real world we inhabit. I personally believe in it, but would make an additional suggestion: perhaps the superstring they are speaking of is actually a 'thoughtstring'.

It is my contention that our universe is bathed in the tangible thoughts of the past, present and future, thus explaining how we develop complex minds and bodies comprising billions of intelligent communicating cells. The elements that make up the physical body comprise energy fields that contain these thoughts and thus know how to form compounds and complexes with other elements to make living forms. This explains all sorts of mysterious natural phenomena such as how sense perception works in animals: how birds, for example, find their way from one part of the world to the other, over thousands of miles, using thought navigation inherent within their bodies and inherent within the land they fly over.

The hundredth monkey

Have you ever strayed into an old house or a ruined castle, thought to yourself, 'there are bad vibrations in here', and then some time later been told about sinister events that once took place within the building? Thoughts can cling to walls and structures; they become embedded in the elements that make up that building. Places can hide horrible faces in the form of unseen thought patterns; by the same token, you can enter a house and feel happy and comfortable with the joyous thoughts that reside in the room. Both animals and humans can communicate with one another through transference of thought. Thoughts already exist; they are not ours. They surround us; we just tap in and listen to them. That's how we as humans and the cells within our bodies know what to do. We are all thought-driven.

This also explains why we get sudden insights into problems we are dealing with; our intuition picks up a thought that already exists with the answer to the question. And this is why group consciousness works, not only in human populations but also in the animal world. If enough people think about a question for long enough, others will pose the same question and will be given the same answer. Inventors often come up with the same ideas for this reason, even though they are on different sides of the planet.

The thoughtstring theory also goes a long way towards explaining the 'one hundredth monkey phenomenon' outlined in many books (including those of Dr Lyall Watson, of *Supernature* fame) on the natural abilities of animals.

This experiment, conducted some years ago, involved a small group of islands inhabited only by monkeys. Scientists decided to test the intelligence of the monkeys by feeding them sweet potatoes and bananas, visiting the islands daily to fill up the bins of food, much to the monkeys' delight. Once the monkeys had established the habit of eating from the bins, the scientists then hid the food in the usual bins but covered and concealed them under dirt and soil. The monkeys were observed to leave the bins and go back into the trees to feed. However, the scientists visited the islands daily and after a few days noticed that on one island the monkeys were reaching into the bins, taking the food, then washing it in the sea before eating it.

After witnessing this on one island the scientists found the monkeys on the other islands were still ignoring the bins and eating from their natural habitat. However, on this one island the monkeys were washing the food and still enjoying the luxury of their food being delivered daily. One day the scientists counted 100 monkeys all washing the food and feeding, but just on this one island. When they visited the many other islands the next day they found, to their amazement, that all the monkeys had come out of the trees and were washing and feeding on the food from the bins.

They repeated the experiment time and time again by testing other sites, with other animals, and kept getting the same result. When 100 or more animals think of an idea to overcome a problem all other similar animals think of it at the same time, however far apart they are (even when they are separated by miles of water). These animals seemed to be listening to the thought patterns existing around them. In the same way, we are surrounded by thoughts containing information about the past. These 'past thoughts' form our instinctual behaviour, 'present thoughts' help us solve problems, and 'future thoughts' give us our intuition.

An invisible force

Apart from genetically inherited diseases and malfunctions, we humans get sick because we have forgotten to listen to the correct thoughts both within and around us. Ask yourself how many times a day you question a thought. Seldom, I imagine. Similarly, do you ever wonder where this or that idea came from? Was it your idea, or was it mine? Do thoughts arise within our minds? Or do we receive them from some other source within our bodies? And are we actually affected by the thoughts of others around us? We seem to go about our daily lives blindly accepting the thoughts and ideas that are the origins of all our actions.

The power of thought processes and the act of thinking, and their effects upon the human organism in terms of health and illness, have largely been ignored by conventional medicine. However, the term 'mind–body medicine' is used by many complementary practitioners to convey the important role of thought, not only in the healing process, but also as a causative factor acting at a very profound level in our conscious and subconscious minds.

Consider the autonomic nervous system. Is it actually a thought that travels through the nerve fibres from the stomach to the brain, for example, and says: 'Hey listen, we have a problem down here. This pain you're experiencing is not serious as yet. But get your brain into action to assist with some physical remedy or just stop worrying so much, and the pain will go away.'? Thoughts that travel through the nervous system seem to carry messages that our brains can unravel into language; they are not just signals passing down a nerve fibre.

It is only when our bodies are sick, or not performing at their best, that thoughts arise within the mind and we wonder whether the symptoms experienced are perhaps the start of an illness, and a visit to the doctor might be necessary.

Perhaps there is a lack of a particular nutrient, vitamin, mineral or other supplement within our daily diet that would aid recovery. Maybe a little patience and observation of the body's natural healing ability is all that is necessary (something very few people think of these days). Often it is difficult for patients to accept the required dietary changes. But then they see for themselves the changes in their symptoms.

This phenomenon raises the following questions: How do our bodies know what to do? And what is within the cells of our bodies that has the intelligence and power to heal, or even to alert our minds to the problem in the first place? As I have previously mentioned, when we injure or cut ourselves we are not consciously aware of the unseen processes that immediately swing into action: the blood coagulates only at the site of the wound; special cells suddenly appear to fight infection; and other innate healing processes begin working automatically, all without our conscious intervention.

This fact alone must encourage us to believe in the existence of a potent force we cannot see, feel or touch. This force probably plays the most important role of all within our existence, and within the existence of all living matter – whether animal, vegetable or mineral. In recent times, there has been much discussion regarding the human mind and medicine, and the power of the mind over the body. For example, there are a number of cancer treatment techniques that are based purely upon visualisation and the focusing of the mind. It is of course impossible to actually observe these methods in practice, apart from seeing a patient in a serene state. One can only witness the resultant effects if the patient's condition improves. When these techniques are successful I believe the patient must be tapping into the unseen energetic force fields of the mind, as well as the minute controlling processes of the cells within the physical body.

The plague of fear

The most common detrimental influences on the body in today's world are stress, anxiety, fear and apprehension. Many of us seem to have a rather negative outlook on life, and this plays havoc with the physical body. Yet most people are unaware of the power of their negative thoughts to change the way cells behave in their bodies.

Wherever you are at this moment, reading this book, imagine an event suddenly taking place that is the stuff of your worst nightmare. Perhaps there would be a sudden scream of absolute terror from another room in the house – an adrenaline rush second to none would flood your bloodstream, preparing you for flight or fight. Yet all these immense internal chemical reactions in your body would be caused by pure thought. No chemical would enter your body to trigger them.

Thought is itself a subtle energy which can actually cause a measurable chemical reaction. In fact, as we have seen, the very act of thinking has many and varied repercussions in the body – it can cause changes in the blood supply, and alter blood pressure and pulse rate. However, probably the most powerful types of thought, when it comes to illness, are those of fear and anxiety. Fearful thoughts can weaken the constitution and lower the defences of the immune system. For a patient, fear is hard to escape. It's the fear of being called back for a further breast scan. It's the fear of being asked for a second cervical smear test. It's the fear one feels when the man in the white coat says: 'I am sorry but it's cancer.'

Of course, organic disease can be attributed to factors other than thought, but the crucial role played by thought in maintaining health or developing ill-health is too great to be ignored. We must learn to manage stress if we are to stay healthy. Many people are subjected to anxiety, worry and fear in their normal working day. Fear of unemployment and lack of fulfillment in the workplace can lead to a lack of interest in our surroundings; this may well lead to complacency, which in turn will affect the way our bodies perform.

All these factors, if present for long periods of time, eventually lead to illness, as the negative thoughts affect the functioning of the body's cells and change the nutritional and absorption processes that keep the body healthy. Thought is all-powerful; use it for your own good, rather than ill.

Some years ago, when I lived and worked in Africa, I heard an ancient Arab tale in which Pestilence met a caravan on the desert road to Baghdad.

'Why are you going to Baghdad?' asked the Arab in charge of the caravan. 'To take five thousand lives,' replied Pestilence.

On the way back from the city the paths of Pestilence and the caravan crossed once more.

'You told me a lie,' protested the Arab angrily to Pestilence. 'Instead of five thousand lives you took fifty thousand.'

'That is untrue,' replied Pestilence. 'I told you no lie. I said I would take five thousand lives and that is all I took, not one more or less. It was *fear* that killed the rest.'

Chapter Six

THE CORRECT TRAIN OF THOUGHT

C HEMOTHERAPY can save the lives of many cancer patients, yet with many others it is ineffectual and they die. Alternative and complementary medicine can both cure and provide an improved quality of life for many cancer patients, yet in other cases it's totally ineffectual and they die. What a conundrum medical practitioners face – all disease is curable but not all patients.

Why should this be? I believe it is because the cause of so many degenerative illnesses lies at a deep and very subtle level in the formative structures of atoms and elements that make up the physical form. It does not matter what type of medicine is used for a patient or for what type of illness; if the cause of the condition is not addressed the patient will not fully recover.

The subtle causes of illness are initially induced by stress and by thought processes that interfere with the atomic structures within cells. Thoughts of fear, anxiety, depression and despondency, along with dissatisfaction with one's life, are the ones that need reversing; otherwise illness will remain. Achievement of our optimum potential in life is essential for maximum well-being.

In endeavouring to achieve our optimum potential in life and enjoy satisfaction from what we accomplish on a day-to-day basis, we have to be on the right life path. In this materially driven age this is almost impossible for the majority of people. Occasionally I meet a patient who admits to being totally happy and at peace with their life and their relationships, but these encounters are few and far between. There are two possible reasons for this. Firstly, those with a role and satisfactory purpose to their lives rarely become sick and have no need to visit a practitioner. Secondly, all the thousands of patients I have seen over the years somehow ended up on the wrong life path or developed incorrect attitudes and thoughts that led to their illnesses. My role is to put them back on the right track, with the correct train of thought.

Putting the power of thought into practice

Those patients of mine who have attained better health all made conscious efforts and were successful in changing their thoughts and attitudes towards their personal worries and anxieties. Many had personalities that were incompatible with their personal or professional environments or even their chosen careers. Obviously, one cannot suddenly change a career or intervene with personal relationships.

However, one *can* establish the cause of the patient's ills, discuss these possible causes, and offer advice on how to develop thoughts and attitudes that will enhance the efficacy of the therapies being used. This type of advice is perfectly compatible with patients taking orthodox drugs or having surgical procedures and likewise those opting for alternative medicine. Patients who have experienced the power of the mind in improving their health have also gained an understanding of how the subtle forces of thought can physically change the body's metabolism.

I often ask patients to participate in a few simple exercises to demonstrate the concept of the mind being all-powerful. Here's one for you to try right now:

- Find yourself a place that is relatively quiet where you can concentrate without too much difficulty.
- Clear your mind of any outside noise or disquiet and cast your thoughts back to the happiest event that has ever happened in your life. Just think about it for a moment. Did a smile come to your face? Did you recall the smiles on the faces of other people, if there were others involved? Did the experience briefly change your heart rate? If any of these changes occurred, you now know that your thoughts and memories of past events can affect you physically today.
- Now cast your mind back to the saddest time in your life. Think about it in some detail. Was it the loss of someone close to you – a good friend or family member? Maybe it was an experience that caused you a lot of grief at the time. Did a tear come to your eye? Did you feel a lump in your throat? If so, this experience of a past emotion, no matter how many years ago, can clearly still affect you today.

Having understood that past events can cause a physical reaction today when recalled from the memory bank of thought, there is another exercise I would like you to experience. This one relates to our perception of everyday reality:

- As you sit or lie quietly reading these words, try to experience a moment in time. Say to yourself, quietly or out loud, the word – 'now'.
- By the time you have finished making the sound of the word, things will already have changed: the shadows in the room, the sounds outside, the position of your body, the movement of a leg or hand. That particular tangible reality of space and time in the room, or wherever you are at the moment, can never ever be experienced again.

This exercise shows that we cannot break time into small enough parts to stop and experience physical time in any detached manner. By the time we have said a word, taken a breath or moved a muscle, that particular event has gone, never to be repeated in an identical fashion. Reality does not stand still long enough for us to perceive its dimensions, let alone our own place in it. There is only one dimension where we can perceive and experience events in the past, and that is the mind.

Entering the space–time continuum

In the mind, with its attendant thoughts and memory bank, we can recall events from the past and actually experience the emotions and physical effects of an event, even though we cannot physically create the environment in which a past event took place. We might travel to the venue where the event took place, but we cannot create the exact conditions in regard to sound, temperature, lighting and, of course, the actual time. We cannot experience the true reality of a past event twice – except in the mind.

Here, in the mind, we can enter the 'space–time continuum'. We can experience the emotion of a past event; we can visualise its excitement or sadness. We can go back in time with our mind's eye during visualisation and feel the effect in our physical body. This ability is of vital importance. We must acknowledge that an unseen and immeasurable thought from the mind can display itself tangibly in the physical body. As we have seen, it can raise blood pressure, alter our heart rate, or make us break out in a cold sweat. Thought is not governed by Einstein's relativity theories. As shown by the EPR experiment, thoughts travel faster than the speed of light and are not confined by space or time. The act of thinking and experiencing the emotions of past events goes beyond the bounds of space–time.

If thoughts of the past affect the physical body, thoughts about the future can have the same effect. There are no limits when it comes to what you can envisage and make happen in the physical body. Therefore it becomes perfectly possible to think or visualise a required change to the body functions, the increase of immune cells, or the removal of a known cause of an illness.

When patients do not understand the power of their thoughts, the negative ones cause illness but usually remain undiagnosed. Negative thoughts of the past and present will cause the endocrine and organ systems to react, producing hormones and other chemical changes in the body that lead to illness. All branches of medicine accept this phenomenon. Therefore all branches of medicine should also accept that visualisation and altered thought processes can have positive physical effects. Medicine cannot embrace one train of thought about physical symptoms emanating from past events without conceding that effects can also manifest from thoughts of future events.

We all know, from personal experience, that the power of the mind transcends time and the body. I have witnessed the effects of controlled thought in action many times. For example, I have seen my children playing together, and witnessed a fall, a bloodied knee or a crack on the head by a ball, but play goes on, their engrossing thoughts of the game excluding the sensation of pain. But when the game is over and they are called in for supper suddenly there is a cry of pain: 'Mummy, my head hurts and my knee's bleeding.' Concentrated thought upon the game allowed the subconscious mind to deal with the messages of pain travelling through the nervous system from the site of the wounds and prevented these sensations entering the conscious mind.

Likewise, emotions of the past can cause a tear to come to your eye, fear will induce adrenaline release, and stress can bring about an altered heart rate. But if your mind can adequately deal with the pain it will not disturb your current train of thought. So, manipulating your thought processes can give you a powerful healing capacity. To exploit this natural energetic force, you need an appreciation of visualisation techniques. The aim is to visualise your future goals and ambitions, and rid yourself of the causative elements that produced your physical symptoms.

Getting rid of the cause

My patients usually receive a prescription of natural remedies and supplements at their initial consultation. Additionally, if appropriate, I provide visualisation techniques. These are based upon keeping the patient on the right track by using the correct train of thought. This procedure is twofold and can be practised and experienced literally as a train journey, or visualised in the mind by those patients suffering immobility.

For example, I have a patient called Victoria who was left to bring up three children with little financial assistance. Her marriage ended many years ago, but her ex-partner still manages to influence the children even though they are now young adults. This caused Victoria considerable stress, producing physical symptoms of muscular pains, exhaustion and headaches.

The continual negative influence exerted by the previous partner clearly had to be erased or cut off. So I told Victoria to write her name on the left-hand side of a piece of plain paper, and the first name only of her previous partner on the right-hand side of the paper. She then drew a line below each name right across the paper, joining the two names together. I asked her to think of the distressing events that had caused the rift between them and, whilst holding these thoughts, told her to take some scissors and cut the paper in half.

Having cut through the line joining the names together, thus making two pieces of paper with a name on each, the next part of the exercise required her to take a short train journey. Victoria took the piece of paper with her ex-partner's name and caught a train from her home town (where all the unhappiness and stress had occurred) to the next stop along the line. She alighted on the platform, consciously screwed up the piece of paper with the partner's name, and placed it in a rubbish bin. I told her to say quietly to herself: 'That's the end of the connection both mentally and emotionally, along with all the influence he exerts upon the family.'

She then crossed to the opposite platform and took a train back home, leaving the thoughts of unhappiness and stress and the name of the cause on that piece of paper. She returned to her home station free of the causes of her mental, emotional and physical ills. Victoria still gets the odd bout of tiredness and stress, as we cannot erase all the memories of the past from our minds, but she always deals with it by visualising the train journey that put her back on track to well-being.

For patients who are immobile the same procedures can be visualised. If you have an illness that is detailed in Part Two of this book, and you can identify both the possible causes and the thoughts that will assist in the healing of your symptoms, then hold these in your mind as you embark on your journey of renewal. If you know what stressful event caused the illness from which you suffer, write it down on a piece of paper, as you will want to leave this in a rubbish bin before you return to your home town, thus ridding yourself of the cause.

I have known patients to associate many and varied articles with possible causes of illness in their lives – perhaps a small gift given to them by a previous partner, an ornament, or even a greetings card. All these symbols of past distress can be discarded before embarking upon their return journey to their home station and renewed well-being.

Such rituals are nothing new. I have heard tales of tribes in South Africa who, when faced with locust swarms destroying their crops, would capture one of the intruders, carefully wrap it in leaves and make a miniature boat from a piece of fallen tree. Carefully, they would float the small symbolic vessel away from their land, taking the intruder away, and – sure enough – the swarm would soon be gone. If no waterway existed nearby then the offending insect was taken away by a tribesman to another area where no crops were grown but food existed for the swarm. Traditional cultures always accepted that God's creatures existed for a reason and would ask them to live elsewhere, enabling the tribe to have sufficient for themselves. The knowledge that thoughts could be transferred from one living organism to another was commonplace amongst ancient peoples. Why should we not utilise this knowledge now?

Visualising yourself well

To visualise renewed health you must have the *correct train of thought* so that you can rid yourself of the causative factors that started your illness. If you are unaware of the cause, use the guidelines given in Part Two under the relevant illness, and imagine yourself standing on the platform of a railway station waiting for a train. Imagine this station is next to a beautiful lake and that across the lake is another station – you can just see it in the distance across the water. The track skirts the shore, taking you on a short journey around the lake to the far station and back again.

Imagine boarding the train, taking with you the thoughts of the events that caused your illness, or – better still – taking with you the symbols or piece of paper with the cause written on it. Enjoy the journey around the lake and when the train stops at the next station, get off and take your symbol to the nearest rubbish bin. Consciously deposit it in the bin and return to the platform.

Now imagine boarding the next train, which takes you further around the lake and back to your home station, where you alight from the train, regenerated, renewed, and free of your burden. You have consciously left the cause of your illness behind.

I tell patients to imagine themselves dressed in beautiful clothes (ones they have always fancied wearing) and see themselves looking fit and well. If patients have skin rashes I tell them to see their skins clean and clear. I tell asthma patients to see themselves breathing deeply and easily as they make their journeys. If patients are immobile I ask them to imagine riding a bicycle to the station to make their particular journey. The important point is to rid yourself of the known cause of your illness, leave it somewhere else, and return to your home station just as you would like to be seen or as you have always imagined yourself.

Children can be assisted on their journey to renewed health by parents telling them a story about a train journey. They can become the railway children who felt unwell, then went off on an exciting adventure, and returned home, leaving their illness behind them at another station.

Children particularly love the 'pink bubble'. Tell your children to imagine themselves inside a large pink bubble, like a giant transparent ball. Once inside, they can safely float around the room or outside on an exiting journey, leaving behind all their pain and discomfort. This works very well when children cannot go to sleep at bedtime.

Imagination and visualisation are so important in ridding yourself of worries and physical illness. Imagine yourself sitting in a comfortable chair and hold in your mind the thoughts and attitudes that you have read in this book that are the possible causes of your physical symptoms or mental worries. Repeat to yourself and then hold in your mind the words you have read under the specific heading of the illness from which you suffer.

Then think of a recent event from your own life that you feel triggered similar emotions to those you have read about under the specific heading. Picture the past event happening and the people you know who were involved with that event at the time.

Once you have considered the causes of your current symptoms, think about reversing them with the healing thoughts and attitudes described. Include the same people and places, but now imagine the situation completely changed – with you having changed your thoughts, actions and attitudes. Perhaps it was a time when you were bullied as a child or when a relationship broke up. Whatever the situation, you need to replace your feelings of fear, pain and grief with positive thoughts of being in control and accepting change.

Now is the time to use these changed attitudes and make them an aspiration for the future. Tell your body, and the millions of cells that listen to your every word, exactly what you desire of them for your future health.

Irrespective of your illness, age or gender, imagine yourself getting up from the chair and going over to the wardrobe. Select the clothes you feel you would like to be seen in if you were *completely* fit and healthy and had no illness whatsoever. Choose the clothes based upon what you would genuinely like to do today, as you really are feeling very healthy. Maybe you would like to go shopping, take a bike ride, go to the beach, take a walk in the woods, or go for a drive in a fast open-top sports car.

Imagine putting on your selected clothes and look at yourself in the mirror. If you had a skin rash it is now gone. If you had a tumour in your lung you are now breathing easily and you are going for a fun run. Whatever illness you had is now gone and the clothes you have chosen to wear today reflect you in a state of perfect health. Spend as much time as you like in your newfound world of health and happiness, and experience your changed attitudes and sense of renewal.

Repeat these visualisation techniques as often as you wish.

Think of them as an additional method of healing your body, whether you have undergone surgery or are about to have any other form of invasive therapy such as radiation. Whether you are having chemotherapy or taking prescribed drugs, they will benefit you. Likewise, patients on alternative or complementary medical therapies will gain from visualisation. These techniques use your positive mental energy to change the way the cells of your body are behaving. The correct thoughts from your mind will restore the natural structures and processes within the cells, thus creating healthy tissue and organs, and restoring health and happiness.

I have selected the various ailments listed in Part Two because they are conditions that complementary medical practitioners and GPs treat most frequently. Once a patient has a diagnosis, they can use the advice given to assist the healing process. Over the many years I have been in complementary practice, I have been consulted for just as wide a range of ailments as a GP would face on a daily basis. However, I use only natural remedies, coupled with an individually designed stress management program for each patient. Just remember that the correct attitude of mind is essential, irrespective of the seriousness of the illness or the type of therapy being administered.

Part Two

An A-Z of Mental, Emotional and Physical Ailments

The following entries contain general information on healing thoughts, vitamin and mineral supplements, and other remedies which have proved effective for these conditions. However, if you are suffering from a particular ailment you should always consult a qualified practitioner (whether conventional or alternative) for detailed advice on treatment and appropriate dosage. For suppliers of supplements and guidance on finding suitable complementary medical practitioners, see Useful Addresses.

ACNE

Acne is a very common skin problem. It usually affects young adults around the time of puberty and can continue well into adult life. It is most prevalent on the face and upper back, with the appearance of red spots or whiteheads and blackheads.

Many doctors prescribe antibiotics to reduce bacterial infection and inflammation. However, treatment often lasts for up to six months and the long-term use of antibiotics can damage the digestive tract. It is well-known that acne often clears up in young adults, once meaningful relationships are established and puberty is fully developed. There are some alternative approaches that may help, mainly the use of vitamins A, C and E. Do not squeeze the spots; allow them to dry out and the inflammation will reduce naturally.

Dietary intake can contribute to skin disorders, and with acne it is particularly the over-indulgence in dairy products, fizzy drinks and sugars. The liver secretes fatty acids that frequently exit through the skin. This is why ointments often do not work and skin conditions are best treated from the inside. In addition there are thoughts that are deleterious and promote a poor skin; these are related to feelings of reluctance to accept change, leading to thoughts of personal inadequacies. Young adults who find themselves facing the world without the support they previously received from parents may wish that things could be as they were in the past. Perhaps they regret the loss of comfortable surroundings and rituals such as family mealtimes. Worries about career choice and general apprehension about the future are other causes. Remember, always speak about your worries.

The way to overcome these thoughts and to give additional healing to the skin, to promote good circulation in the skin cells and cleanse the old thoughts, is to develop a purpose in life. Decide what you are going to do, make a decision and stick to it for a few years at least. Have the strength and courage to face the new world you see before you, take the opportunities that come your way and genuinely believe in your own capabilities. Try to create order within your daily life and less chaos, though it's OK to take a calculated risk from time to time. Look in the mirror each day and congratulate yourself on how good you look.

ADDICTIONS

Addictions can be both acute (as in the use of items on a periodic basis) and chronic (as in addiction to drugs, either prescribed or illegal). In addition there are the everyday addictions to alcohol and tobacco that become habitual and compulsive. Hobbies and interests can also become addictive. Addictions are similar to obsessions in that they are often used by people to divert attention away from a personal inadequacy.

∾

Conventional medicine often uses counselling techniques to wean a patient off an addictive substance, or uses drugs to reduce the craving by inducing a calming of the brain and central nervous system. Alternative techniques of visualisation and psychotherapy are very successful. However, the cause of the initial use of the addictive substance needs to be found. And by addressing the cause, the addiction is often cured more quickly and more permanently.

Patients with addictions of any type need to respond actively to challenges on a daily basis, as addiction is often caused by a reluctance to withstand a challenge or face a certain reality in life. Addicts must learn to rely upon themselves and their own judgement and less upon the help of other people, particularly family members. People who suffer from addictions will often choose the easy way out of situations, rather than tackle the problem or difficulty. People who have had life easy from the start, those with an inheritance who are not required to work or to make ends meet, will often become addicts as their inner personality and natural inclination to develop a purpose in life are suppressed. Their instinctive energies will demand a release; and addiction will become a regular ritual in order to satisfy their inner need for a purpose in life.

Strict codes of practice should be adhered to by any addict and a traditional framework of life developed. Things should be done according to a schedule and daily life should follow a pattern. Avoid temptation and spend less time alone – mix with people who are full of ideas and are always busy. In personal relationships, allow others to rely more upon you for strength when *they* are emotionally upset and need a shoulder to rest upon. The more responsibility you accept, the less you will require the addictive substance.

Take a long hard look at the positive qualities and attributes you have, or had in the past; rekindle the flame in your personality and make your light shine out to others. Make sure the positive assistance you give others is noticed, but do not seek any reward; this will come from your inner satisfaction as the obsession lessens and your addiction decreases. Think about those you may have unintentionally hurt in the past, make contact and make amends. Realise that others around you, who adhere to differing beliefs and codes of behaviour from your own, are actually progressing along their own path of life.

AGORAPHOBIA

Agoraphobia is a morbid dread of open spaces or of being in crowds or even crossing the street. The cause of these symptoms has not been clearly defined but it normally arises after prolonged periods of stress and nervous tension.

Treatment for agoraphobia is usually by drugs classified as benzodiazepines; these are effective for the short-term relief of nervousness and tension. However, these types of drugs can become addictive if taken regularly over longer periods than are normally recommended, and the effects become weaker over time. Alternative medicine, with the use of homeopathy and Dr Bach flower essences, can be very effective.

❧

Fear is one of the main causes of agoraphobia, along with feelings of insecurity. The opposite of fear is love and it is often the case that those who are unlucky in love become fearful of the future and insecure with their feelings which may have been hurt. The events that caused the phobia or fixation must be left behind and the future entered with confidence and courage; this will drive out the fear. Sometimes the loss of someone very close will cause panic attacks, as one feels life is never going to be the same again.

These days, love is always linked to relationships, and our understanding of one another in relationships is always linked to love. In this context love becomes more than just an emotional or physical attraction to another person. Understanding another person's needs enables one to learn through love, and learning how to give and receive love in return is very important. Those who become devoted to another but do not receive the same affection in return will develop fear and inner repression of their emotions.

The way forward in overcoming agoraphobia is to display calmness. Imagine yourself in a situation of peace and quiet where you can experience tranquillity of mind and body. Try to experience this when visualising the changes you need in your life. Feel the tranquillity of your train journey when you leave the baggage of life behind at the station; return with inner peace to your home stop.

Become a person with high ideals, couple this with strength in your personality, and be an example to those you share your life with, as this will also enhance the lives of others around you. People who suffer from agoraphobia are normally faithful, patient and kind to others, and it seems unjust that they should suffer so much torment and lack of understanding.

ANAEMIA

The main function of red blood cells is to transport life-giving oxygen around the body. A reduction in the number of red cells or haemo-globin to below normal levels is referred to as anaemia. There are many and various causes of anaemia, from excessive blood loss during periods to inadequate diet, or bone marrow and kidney disorders. Your doctor can examine you and carry out blood tests to establish if anaemia exists and can prescribe iron supplements if required.

∾

A diet rich in iron, vitamin B12 and folic acid will overcome most anaemic conditions (such foods are liver and lamb, and for non-meat eaters, green leaf vegetables, dried apricots and dates), but there are other causes. I have witnessed cases of anaemia and other symptoms related to blood disorders developing in people without dietary deficiencies. Some patients expect high ideals and integrity from others (similar to their own). If these are not forthcoming they feel inner resentment and sometimes anger due to the actions of others. Anger, as a negative emotion, appears to affect the absorption of iron. Enforced changes in people's lives, at a time when they themselves appear happy in an environment, will also upset the stability of the blood. The circulation of blood in the body takes nutrition to the whole biological system and removes the waste; therefore it is important to have a balanced environment, both internal and external.

If your environmental balance is disrupted due to the actions of others, try to develop an understanding that everyone behaves in a manner that is correct for them at a particular time. To enforce change upon others, due to your own desires, will not always bring the results you want.

Concentrate on developing a calmer nature, assist others when things go wrong for them and imagine, when doing visualisation exercises, being a focal point of support and assistance for others. Developing attitudes of caring and understanding for humanity appears to help disorders of the bloodstream.

ANGER

Anger arises from feelings of bitterness and resentment, often due to enforced changes in one's life direction. The anger can occur because of one's non-acceptance of change, or due to the actions of others. Anger comes from the frustration caused by not being able to rectify matters and depression is often a result.

The feelings accompanying anger will normally be treated with anti-depressants which do relieve symptoms but do very little to rectify the underlying problem or encourage patients to seek out the cause of their anguish.

In the course of life we are all at some point faced with apparently unpleasant change. But the events that lead to the alteration of circumstances are often necessary in order that we should progress along the path of life. Non-acceptance of change is a retrogressive step; if the patient refuses to even consider the possibilities offered by those helping them this can cause loneliness to develop. The combination of these feelings brings about fear for the future and the anger can actually lead to an illness developing at a physical level.

If you find you are reluctant to face the cause of the anger within and are clinging to things you have outgrown (whether people or material possessions), maybe it's time to cut the ties that bind. The enforced change may be necessary to sever your attachment. However, the emotion of anger causes disorders of the blood supply, so look at the entries for **angina** and **blood pressure** as these may also apply. Try to develop some inner peace and rapport with those around you, both in personal relationships and at work.

ANGINA

Angina is a temporary pain or tightness that starts in the middle of the chest and may spread to the back, neck, upper jaw and often the left arm. Pains are heavy, rather than sharp or piercing. Like other muscles in the body, the heart needs adequate supplies of oxygen, and when blood vessels are narrowed they cannot supply the required oxygen fast enough. The pain experienced is actually due to the heart muscle becoming short of oxygen.

∽

Your doctor can prescribe both tablets and a spray to use during an attack and you can consult a practitioner in complementary medicine who is qualified in nutrition to supply you with advice about magnesium, as this element is always required in angina cases. Dietary sources of magnesium are green leafy vegetables, nuts (except for patients who are allergic to them), and wholemeal cereals, soya beans and seafood. Irrespective of the therapy used for your condition, the following thoughts and attitudes will also be of benefit – along with deep breathing and gentle exercise.

Angina occurs when there is a lack of elasticity in the body and, as the heart is a muscle which is experiencing spasm and tension, you need to develop more flexibility in your life. Thoughts of enmity, bitterness and stubbornness will harm you. Sometimes your obstinate ways cause you to miss important opportunities and this can lead to resentment or jealousy of the success that others achieve. Try to be more adaptable and diplomatic when dealing with others, and listen openly to their views and opinions. Do not be timid in your approach to others, and likewise do not be intimidated by their strong convictions and wilfulness.

Try to be less rigid, look at yourself as others may see you, and step back and review the criticism in a constructive manner. A more relaxed attitude will relax the muscles; and your heart is nothing more than a muscle. Release your inner stresses and speak more freely to others about your worries and anxieties. Do not secretly hold on to your fears, and do not be fearful of the hospital, the doctor or the dentist.

Try to face these fears and decide what it is that causes them. It may be a past event. If so, leave it in the past and release these fears from your heart. Flexible and adaptable thinking will heal. Unwind and relax the tension – perhaps even try some meditation (see Useful Addresses).

ANOREXIA

Lack of or even a complete loss of appetite often arises from a nervous cause. However, lack of absorption from adequate diet can also lead to symptoms classified as anorexia and help should be sought from a qualified nutritionist. Patients suffering these symptoms due to a nervous complaint or from shock and trauma will need assistance from both good nutrition and counselling.

∾

To cause the body suffering by lack of nutrition often signals a lack of desire for life. However, this condition also often arises from a subconscious intention engendered by events that have affected the mind in a very subtle manner, often a stress or trauma of long standing. Medical treatment for these types of symptoms differs according to each individual case. My treatment is aimed at reducing nervous anxiety and tension, along with some dietary advice.

Some years ago I had a typical example of a patient who had suffered a major trauma in her life and the experience had caused her to lose sight of the wonderful inner qualities she possessed that could help her overcome the effects of the shock. Vicky came to see me about two years ago: she was thirty-two years old, going through a divorce and weighed just 77 pounds even though she was 5 feet 6 inches tall.

Vicky had been diagnosed anorexic and was not responding to orthodox treatment. My initial aim was to establish the cause of this weight loss and apparent lack of desire to live, though I knew there was a spark of life within her as she had come to see me of her own accord and not at anyone else's insistence. Vicky completed the twenty or so questions on the questionnaire and I put the information into my computer, as I wanted to know more about her general constitution and her true personality. (These aspects are very difficult to establish from a patient when they feel so wretched.) This is what the program produced as written text for Vicky:

> You are a person with certain ideals, and certain moral standards, and in your relationships both at a personal and business level you will display calmness and a general strength of character, with honesty. This honesty will show through as an example to those you choose to share your life with, and in turn this example will enhance the lives of those you are close to. Patience, kindness and understanding, particularly of the needs of others, and your love of humanity as a whole make you a person of truth and integrity. Intuition is a strong element within your personality, and this gives you clear insights into problems or difficult situations that confront you on a day-to-day basis. Your clear intellect enables you to act at the right time; there is innate knowledge as to when to act. When dealing with new ventures or projects there is also an inner wisdom. Sometimes you even think to yourself: I know how to do this.
>
> Considering your attributes of love, patience, and the understanding of others' needs, it is very important that during your lifetime you also receive from those close to you the same love and understanding in return.
>
> If this is not forthcoming, it can manifest as inner frustration and even resentment, not only of those close to you, but of humanity in general, particularly those with substantial financial assets, turning itself into jealousy.

A few months before Vicky fell ill she had discovered her husband was being unfaithful. Coupled with this, she had found that a close friend and work colleague was acting dishonestly within the accounting firm where she was employed. Vicky was faced with two major dilemmas. Firstly, she loved her husband yet did not receive the same love and affection in return. Secondly, she knew the work colleague should be reported but she felt reluctant to do so and kept quiet. Vicky became very nervous, her thyroid was affected, and her basal metabolism severely disrupted, to the point where she lost tissue and muscle tone and anorexic symptoms were established. Because of these events, Vicky no longer used the strengths of her caring and loving personality. Instead, she naturally became very bitter and jealous.

The bitterness was reflected in her digestion and liver, and the inability to speak her mind affected her thyroid. I instilled into Vicky that, although she felt bitter towards others at present, the way forward was to call upon those inner strengths she had always possessed and they would see her through this terrible time. I encouraged her to accept that all people are different and they act as they see fit at a particular time. I suggested she use the wonderful attributes she had, and I printed out the computer read-out for her to take away and to look at from time to time in order to reinstate her positive attributes. I also prescribed digestive enzymes, mineral supplements and some Dr Bach remedies. On her third visit to my clinic, two months after treatment had begun, she had put on 7 pounds, and the last I heard from Vicky was that she had been promoted and a new relationship was flourishing. One other important note on the case history: I remember Vicky came to my clinic on two occasions wearing all black and dark clothes. I suggested a new and colourful wardrobe, which she agreed to. And many weeks later, when she came for the last time, she was wearing bright and cheerful colours and make-up.

Anorexic symptoms can also result from childhood experiences of inadequacy triggered by harsh words from parents or siblings – feelings of never quite rising to the occasion or standards demanded by others. Severe symptoms include hopelessness and despair of ever becoming well. Try to establish which events caused the inadequate feelings. Is the sense of inadequacy mental, emotional or physical? Learn to love yourself; take a look in the mirror, be proud of what you see and concentrate upon the attributes you know you possess.

Visualisation for this condition must include leaving all your baggage and clutter from the past behind you and imagining yourself in your favourite clothes, looking astounding, when you arrive home after the mediation or journey of rediscovery. The Dr Bach flower essences (see Useful Addresses) are very effective in the treatment of anorexia, because the essences are related to current feelings, some of which may be despondency, despair and the feeling of never ever recovering one's well-being.

Patients who suffer symptoms related to concealing themselves and their appearance will often wear dark or very neutral colours. I often tell these patients to show the world how they can blossom like a spring flower by wearing colourful and attractive clothes. This makes you feel confident and assured in a very short time, just as in Vicky's case. It does wonders for the morale and will have a profound and almost immediate effect upon both the conscious and subconscious mind. Wear these beautiful clothes when you do your meditation or visualisation, and imagine yourself dining at the best restaurant and enjoying the food put before you. Love yourself, love your body, and it will soon demand nutrition to live up to your new demands and the anorexic symptoms will fade.

ANXIETY

Anxiety, depression, despondency and despair are common conditions suffered in this modern Western world as we all strive to make ends meet materially and still endeavour to find some inner peace and tranquillity within ourselves and with our families. A certain amount of stress can be beneficial, providing a stimulus to action. But too much will often result in anxiety, which can be described as fear or apprehension not caused by real or apparent danger. Clinically, anxiety arises when the balance between certain chemicals in the brain is disturbed. The feelings of fear increase brain activity, stimulating the sympathetic nervous system, which triggers physical symptoms such as shaking, palpitations, breathlessness, digestive disturbance and headaches.

∾

A nti-anxiety drugs called anxiolytics, or minor tranquillisers, are used to alleviate the persistent symptoms of nervousness and tension resulting from stress and other psychological problems, but they cannot resolve the causes of the stress.

Doctors will also prescribe anti-depressants, along with beta-blockers, and in cases where insomnia persists sleeping drugs will be prescribed. However, tackling the underlying cause is paramount and is best done through counselling or psychotherapy. Homeopathic medicine and Dr Bach flower essences will also offer relief and in some cases will address the causes. In the case of these treatments, you need to seek professional help from a qualified practitioner in complementary medicine.

Patients suffering anxiety sometimes feel that life is a constant struggle, and many aspects of their personal life are fraught with difficulties. But remember that the struggle is always worth the effort, as the rewards are there at completion. Patients often feel inner conflict, both of an emotional nature, and sometimes at a business level, and this will cause higher than normal levels of stress and trauma. During our lives we all experience events that cause radical changes. Sometimes we consider these changes unwelcome at the time, yet they will clear the way forward after a period of inner conflict, reminding us of our real purpose in life. The emergence from conflict, whether experienced within oneself or externally with others, often coincides with the removal of outdated or superfluous aspects in life, allowing us to move forward into the future unhindered.

Remember that life is the greatest teacher of all. Changes in life often occur as the result of another's actions, and you will think to yourself on many occasions that the stress or trauma emanating from the change was none of your own doing. This will promote inner resentment, but do not dwell on this aspect; it will do you more harm than good, particularly in terms of your health.

Anxiety often causes feelings of lack of confidence, so it is very important for you to develop and enjoy the art of conversation, and to have a sense of humour that will put your friends or work colleagues at ease in your company. When you are going through inner stress or conflict you may experience some depression and you will range from brilliant conversation to sometimes-gloomy silences, depending on your mood at the time. Never forget that you can develop into a delightful person to live with, if at times a little difficult. However, your mood can be instantly changed by a change of clothes. Include decorative and colourful prints in your outfits, as colour will always lighten your mood. Colour will also play an important role in your home life – always surround yourself with colour and light.

To overcome anxiety and depression, you need willpower. This can arise from your own strength of character if used in a selfless manner, for your own further development, and for the benefit of others. We all have an innate physical fight or flight mechanism; at a mental and emotional level, likewise, we tend to persevere when faced with a challenge. But in anxiety and depression the fight or flight mechanism can be weakened, so you need to work on your ability to 'fight' – or face up to challenges. When anxiety persists, your personality will need a challenge in order to respond actively on a daily basis to the feelings you experience. The ability to respond to a challenge leads you to rely upon yourself rather than others to overcome the obstacles you encounter along life's path.

I recall a patient suffering from anxiety and panic attacks when she was faced with life on her own. Her children were now at university, her husband was working in London from dawn till dusk, and she found herself without a role. Panic set in as she paced around her immaculate home, with nothing more to polish or clean. She had very few new goals or ambitions and this is where I started with her treatment. I suggested voluntary work, inviting friends for discussions, starting a reading group and many other ideas to overcome the obstacles she was putting in front of her way ahead. Suddenly she found more to talk about with her husband when he returned home in the evenings. In fact he called me one day and remarked that his wife had become much more interesting to be with. She had taken on a new identity from that of the housewife sitting at home; her life was now so busy she had no time to panic.

When you practise visualisation imagine dealing with those obstacles you see before you. Do not shy away from the goals you have set yourself; keep your eyes on them and the obstacles will soon be cleared. In some cases of anxiety, particularly when change is required, it would be advisable to develop stricter codes and practices coupled with more traditional values in your daily life. It is very important that everything is done decently and in order, and that you become a person who works according to rule, morals and precedent, in both your personal and business life.

As you rise to the above qualities, it is also important to remember that others have their own rights and needs, and that which is right for you may not be right for others. You need to realise that those who adhere to beliefs and codes of behaviour that differ from your own are in fact progressing along their own chosen path in life.

Take a long hard look at your life and environment and address the causes of the anxiety, which may be your intolerance, narrow-mindedness and dogmatism. Facing the realities of your own inner imperfections will take you a long way towards over-coming the anxiety.

ARTHRITIS, RHEUMATOID

Rheumatoid arthritis can be the most crippling and deforming type of arthritis, causing pain, stiffness and swelling of the affected joints due to thickening of the synovial membrane, which increases the fluid around the joint. Osteoarthritis is different in its action, in that the joint and cartilage wear away and become inflamed and painful. Osteoarthritis affects the main weight-bearing joints, whereas rheumatoid arthritis can affect any joint.

◖

D octors will prescribe both anti–inflammatory drugs and steroids to relieve the pain and reduce the swelling, but the causes of arthritis can vary – from mental and emotional stresses to environmental pollutants and dietary problems. Natural supplements, along with vitamins and minerals, can be very effective but it is essential that the stress factors and the thoughts behind the stresses are addressed.

Lack of determination can lead to over–indulgence which can produce arthritic conditions. When life presents you with a challenge it is important to at least make an attempt to overcome the problem. If you lack the courage to conquer the problem or to discuss it and seek advice, you may develop passions or obsessions in a totally different direction as your mind diverts away from the issue at hand.

For example, many patients will continue to eat white bread and pastries, along with regular fried foods, even when advised that this form of diet is damaging to the skeletal metabolism. Arthritis often occurs through dietary deficiencies or excesses and nutritional advice is imperative.

Foods or confectionery that form part of a dietary habit must be eliminated, just like the other desires or obsessions that divert the patient's mind from the causative issues. Take a look at those areas of your life that are different. Look at your habits in comparison with those people who do not suffer arthritic conditions; notice perhaps how much more flexible they are in their attitudes to daily life. If you have habits with certain foods (and I had a patient once who insisted on eating four or five apples every evening and had done so for years), try to refrain from the compulsion. Aim for moderation in all things. When you take a journey or hop on the 'train of thought', leave your obsessions on the other platform and return home with a changed attitude.

Try to be more flexible in your attitudes to diet and also to family members or friends who try to assist you in your healing. Remember flexible actions of the mind will promote flexible actions of the body, so visualise yourself in adaptable moods, and witness other people's reactions as you bend to meet their desires and ideas.

ASTHMA

Asthma is a very common condition and can start at any age. It is often hereditary and it affects over three million people in the UK alone. It is a chronic condition affecting the lungs; it narrows and inflames the minute airways, making it harder to get air in and out of the lungs.

It is more common in people who suffer from eczema and hayfever. Doctors normally prescribe inhalers to relax the muscles around the air passages of the lung, allowing the patient to breathe more easily.

In addition to the known causes of asthma (which include the hereditary factors affecting small children in particular), respiratory illness often occurs in those who have a tendency to worry too much about small, trifling things. In some children it could be triggered by a forced move to another school, a lost friend causing loneliness, or a change in familiar surroundings.

Children hate being left alone and being separated from their parents for any length of time, as lack of security and inner loneliness can trigger an asthma attack. If you have a child suffering from asthma, and that child is old enough to understand, try to convince them that acceptance of change is necessary for progression in life.

One very important factor with asthma sufferers: they should never isolate themselves from their friends or families. In my practice I have treated many asthma sufferers over the years and I have found that intellectuals, in particular, can sometimes develop asthma which in turn leads to absent-mindedness, with a cold, indifferent attitude towards others of lesser knowledge or understanding. This can only manifest further as isolation and loneliness.

A case that springs to mind was that of a well-respected lawyer who had given many years' service to the community. His overall health was excellent and the expansion of his law firm necessitated the appointment of an additional partner. However, the new addition to the firm proved to be a threat to his security, as several of his clients moved to the new associate. My patient found he could no longer express his true feelings and others in the firm would not listen to his viewpoint. He lost long-established clients and felt very lonely amongst his peers. His asthma was initially acute but soon moved into a chronic stage. This was when he consulted me, as the inhalers supplied by his physician were starting to prove less effective.

I gave him natural remedies that provided him with more elasticity in his connective tissue and muscles. In particular, flower essence remedies gave him tolerance of his work situation. I told him to speak more freely about his feelings to his wife and family and to seek out close friends who would listen to the whole story.

My advice was to accept change as part of his own evolution. In this situation within the law firm, he was to use his knowledge to help bring about change. This in turn would bring back his confidence, he would display certitude and conviction, and others would believe once more in his competence. He took my advice and the natural remedies; the asthma went in a few weeks, never to return.

So, try not to lose your nerve when facing day-to-day problems; and be more flexible in coping with enforced changes in your life, whether personal or business. This will lead you to develop a clearer intellect and a more positive attitude, which will allow you to communicate more freely with those around you. Communication is the key to overcoming asthma: do not keep your inner thoughts locked away.

Asthma sufferers have told me they can even feel lonely when in a crowd, so try to communicate more. Don't be shy, talk about what is on your mind, and others will listen.

BACK PAIN

Four out of five people experience back pain at some time throughout their lives. Some have more serious problems with long-term or chronic backache, but apart from these cases more than 25,000 people in the UK will be absent from work for more than one or two days because of an acute back pain.

Backache is commonly caused by poor posture in sitting, driving and standing positions, and when sleeping on soft beds, along with strain through lifting and excess exercise. The muscles and ligaments that hold the spinal column erect can go into spasm, resulting in pressure upon the vertebra which can pinch nerves or cause misalignment of the spine, all of which cause localised pain.

Most doctors will prescribe rest for a couple of days, along with anti-inflammatory drugs and painkillers. Calcium and magnesium supplements are always of benefit for connective

tissue, along with homeopathic medicine. An osteopath or chiro-
practor can also help, but make sure you consult a competent and
registered practitioner (see Useful Addresses).

Back pain sufferers should look at the methods they use to get
things done, not only in the workplace but also at home.
Sometimes your method of conducting life needs to be changed,
because you may need to respond more readily and willingly to
daily events. At times you can be complacent about responding
to challenges; you will sometimes manipulate situations, and allow
others to shoulder responsibility. Letting someone else do more
than their fair share of work, so that you have less to do (particularly in the home), is a common factor in bringing on backache.
For more on back pain and sciatica, see the entry for **migraines**.

It is very important for you to shoulder your own responsibilities but not everyone else's. Most of us have heard of frozen
shoulder, which comes from tension and muscular spasm. There
are some cases of backache where the sufferer is actually shoul-
dering other people's burdens and they do too much to help others.

Summon up the courage to make changes. Persevering at the
job in hand will, in the long run, strengthen your determination
to help others, and yourself along your chosen path of life. Take
time to look at your actions and how you affect the lives of
others. Flexibility and the ability to bend, both mentally and
emotionally, will give pliability to the physical body. Be determined but less rigid, and do not put off until tomorrow what
should be done today. Take full control of your life and rely less
upon others to make decisions for you.

BED-WETTING (nocturnal enuresis)

*This occurs mostly in children from the age of five years onwards, and
is said to be chronic when the child wets the bed at least three nights
per week. Causes arise from negative attitudes from parents or carers,*

particularly when children are punished for bed-wetting and made to feel guilty.

Stress plays a big part as do such factors as going into hospital or a marital breakdown. Your doctor must look at infections of the urinary tract when there is burning on urination.

∾

L oving and caring attitudes, along with confidence–building, will help children over some enuresis but see also the entry on **bladder problems**. For younger, more sensitive patients I have used homeopathic Pulsatilla with some success.

BLADDER PROBLEMS

People with bladder problems are sometimes unable to control their bladders and may release urine at the wrong time. Under normal circumstances the bladder function is consciously controlled, and bladder emptying should take place no more than six or seven times a day and sometimes once at night. People of all ages can have difficulty with controlling bladder function and medical help should be sought if a bladder condition persists, as there are many different types of bladder disorders and causes of urinary incontinence.

∾

I n children, thoughts of anxiety and worry can cause night–time bed-wetting and in the case of adults mental and emotional worries can cause similar problems. As people get older there are often physical factors, involving the whole urinary tract and including the kidneys, which can lead to bladder problems.

For adults and children alike, the less stress or anxiety in life the easier it is to overcome any bladder problems. However, the main factor in this type of condition is the patient's determination. The patient has to have the conscious will to overcome the problem. It is important to listen to the advice of others, as we sometimes see events and their associated stresses differently from others. Any symptom related to the lower back area, affecting the kidneys, adrenal glands or urinary tract, requires determination and willpower to be reinstated within the patient.

Over-indulgence and self-opinionated attitudes are detrimental to bladder sufferers, and any restrictive practices or refusing to give up a point of view or a favourite food or drink will cause additional problems. The refusal to listen to sound advice, and the obstinacy of stumbling headlong into further difficulties, should also be avoided.

Allowing life to flow unhindered, accepting inherent faults and making the necessary changes will help. Participating in life and allowing it to flow with enjoyment is the key. Do not create barriers or blockages, listen to your own inner thoughts as well as the advice and thoughts of others. Take time to stand outside yourself and see how others may perceive your actions and attitudes. If you think change is necessary then make the effort.

BLOOD PRESSURE (high)

Blood pressure is a measurement of the force exerted by the blood circulating in the arteries. Two readings are taken: One indicates force while the heart's ventricles are contracting (systolic pressure). This will be higher than the other reading, which measures the blood pressure during the ventricle relaxation (diastolic pressure). Blood pressure varies among individuals and increases with age. If blood pressure measurements are high on more than three occasions your doctor will prescribe drugs based upon the underlying cause. Most high blood pressure symptoms are treated with beta-blockers, diuretics, vasodilators to enlarge the blood vessels, and drugs to act upon the brain and muscles to prevent constriction of the blood vessels. This type of treatment is classified as anti-hypertensive.

༄

Nutritional advice should be sought for blood pressure problems and supplements containing potassium, magnesium and calcium, along with certain herbal constituents will be of benefit (see Metagenics under Useful Addresses). In addition, reducing stress is essential. Try some yoga or meditation (see Useful Addresses).

There are certain attitudes that heighten blood pressure, such as resentment and bitterness arising from difficulty in dealing with stressful situations. These stresses can arise from being a little too stubborn and dogmatic in your approach to life and the needs of others. This probably stems from the fact that you base your expectations in life on what has already happened to you. Perhaps you concentrate too much on negative aspects, instead of looking at what might have been if your attitude had been a little different and you focused more on the positive side of life.

Affairs of the heart – that is emotional upset and overcaring towards others – can sometimes be an additional factor in blood pressure problems. Many people become devoted to their loved ones over the years, but it is vital for such people to receive the same amount of love in return.

A feeling of resentment and animosity, due to being rejected by loved ones, can be a major problem and will affect the circulation. Allow people to be themselves at all times, but try not to be a martyr in affairs of the heart.

In life it is true to say that 'you reap what you sow'. In this regard, the more you personally put into life, the more you assist others in their plights, and the more you respect the beautiful world we live in and share with all creation, the more you will find fulfilment in your own life. You must also be prepared to take calculated risks and to show initiative. Initiative, when used correctly, can help you overcome known obstacles.

For example, a restaurant owner consulted me some years ago, suffering from high blood pressure that required continual medication. I discovered that he was stressed because his restaurant needed refurbishing and he was unsure about taking the risk of an additional loan. He had been procrastinating for about two years, the same length of time the blood pressure had been elevated.

I suggested he take some professional advice from a person well known in the catering trade. This he did, and, as well as taking some natural medication, he decided to take the calculated risk. The venture succeeded and a few weeks later he called to say his blood pressure was back to normal. This simple case of not wanting to take a calculated risk had caused his blood pressure problem.

Your own positive thinking will help you overcome the hesitation you sometimes experience, and will give you the ability to face reality. Don't hold back, hold your objectives and goals in mind at all times, and do not hold on to negative or bad experiences. Leave them behind at the train station so that you can get back on track.

BLOOD PRESSURE (low)
AND HYPOGLYCAEMIA

Low blood pressure is largely ignored by orthodox medicine as a clinical illness but complementary medical practitioners are aware that this condition can cause many aggravating sets of symptoms, often associated with low or variable blood sugar levels. The two appear to go hand-in-hand, causing hypoglycaemia. Variable blood sugar levels have a similar effect to low blood pressure symptoms, as they disrupt brain function and muscular performance, and cause fatigue, irritability and depression.

∾

L ow blood pressure often occurs when people have inconsistent attitudes. At times patients appear impractical and changeable, sometimes to the point of being contradictory. Depending on their environment at the time, people may switch from brilliant conversation to gloomy silence. There is a need to be more consistent and more flexible in your attitudes. Learn from your experience, and this should give you more self-control in life, and certainly more willpower to get things done.

If you experience low blood pressure, do not keep blaming yourself for everything, including mistakes made by others. Even if things could have gone better do not blame yourself, as this only causes a lack of elasticity in the veins and blocks the supply of blood as it returns to the heart. Lift the despondency that surrounds your inner personality. Learn to bend in the winds of change that continually blow over you, as they will continue to do so throughout your life.

BPH (benign prostatic hyperplasia)

This is the name given to enlargement of the prostate gland, believed to be caused by the effects of male sex hormones. The enlarged gland is about the size of a chestnut; surrounds the tube leading from the bladder and restricts the urine flow. Many men over the age of fifty experience some difficulty in urination because of BPH. However, it is not a cancerous condition even though many symptoms of prostate cancer are similar. It is important to see your doctor about the condition, particularly if you pass blood in semen or urine.

Your doctor will offer drugs to shrink the enlarged gland or to relax the muscles and nerves controlling urine flow. However, there are also some positive alternative steps you can take to improve the condition. At a mental and emotional level, you need to let go of those events that have thwarted your progress in life. Most men suffering prostate conditions have experienced events that have caused them to hold on to emotions rather than to let them go. The thoughts that harm are those that make you think life is never going to be as good as it was in the past; these patients do not think about the inner wisdom and peace that accompany the ageing process.

As the need and in some cases the ability to father children subsides, and as emotional changes occur in relationships with partners experiencing menopause symptoms, it becomes more important for men to look towards the inner wisdom and knowledge they have gained from life. The objective in later life should not be to crave the continuing ability to perform the sexual act but to gain strength and solace from the wisdom of age to be shared with partners and family.

A shift of focus is required for prostate sufferers – away from the sexual organs and the debility of the urinary tract and in some cases impotence, and towards the realisation that life is entering another phase. Many patients of mine have taken up further education, computer courses and new hobbies. One patient became a magistrate and found that his ability to preside over cases, using the knowledge and wisdom gained from life's experiences, caused his prostate to reduce and his impotence to disappear. Do not look back in anger at your life; look forward with certainty.

BREAST LUMPS AND BREAST PAIN

Two out of every three women will experience breast pain at some time in their lives. The medical term for breast pain is mastalgia. Some women suffer cyclic breast pain that occurs several days before the start of the menstrual cycle; other breast pain would be classed as non-cyclic.

Many women worry that their breast pain may be caused by breast cancer. However, breast pain as the only symptom is uncommon. Always check yourself for breast lumps, irrespective of any pains (cyclic or non-cyclic) and if in doubt consult your GP. Always be aware and tell your doctor if your breasts change in shape, or if skin puckering or dimpling occurs. Any discharge or change to the nipple, and any new lumps or discomfort or different type of pain should be reported to your GP or women's clinic.

B reast pain can be helped by taking evening primrose oil for a few months, and if the pain persists your doctor can prescribe painkilling drugs. It is imperative to have breast lumps professionally examined and screened. However, for benign lumps and fibrous tissue in the breast the use of elemental minerals can be very effective. Often the cause of a breast lump is a lack of fibrin in the tissue. This causes the tissue to harden as the fibrin comes out of solution and will also allow calcification to develop. Potassium chloride as a celloid (available from Blackmores – see Useful Addresses) is excellent. Homeopathic remedy of Bryonia is often useful to counteract further lumps.

Having treated women of all ages with breast lumps, I am convinced that there is a very subtle cause at a mental and emotional level that is responsible for their formation. The breast is an organ of motherhood and nourishment for a woman's offspring when young. But in later life the breast will still have this vital energy, even if the hormonal ability to provide nourishment has passed. Mothers use the breast to comfort their children in early years; later it is superseded by hugging the child. It is often when children leave home and move away from a mother's sustenance, good food and subtle vigilance that she feels impotent in her ability to care.

There is much worry and anxiety about the young adult now going out into the big wide world, and the mother no longer feels able to be the guiding sentinel. The mother's breast is no longer a vital symbol in her life and breast lumps often occur as a result of lack of adaptability to changing circumstances. Adaptability and fluidity are essential to prevent the natural fibrin coming out of solution and causing fibrous tissue and breast lumps to develop.

This scenario also applies to women who have not had children. The vital organ of the breast remains, and often the longing for children or the frustration arising from thwarted attempts to have children can lead to a breast lump.

With this condition, the thoughts that harm are lack of adaptability, non-acceptance of change or resentment of your children moving away and out of your care. The healing thoughts are that moving away is a necessary progression for your children; visualise visiting them in their new surroundings and seeing them fit and healthy and enjoying life to the full. This is what mothers should do when their offspring fly the nest.

Women should also recognise how their role in life has changed over the last two decades, from providing the internal home environment for partner and children, to providing additional material support for the family by working outside as well as inside the home. The modern woman has a far greater workload.

Women with breast lumps should develop their authority in another direction by taking on jobs where experience in life counts for a great deal. Working in advice centres and counselling, for instance, will give a new stimulus to their daily lives. Visualise yourself being needed by others, not just by young people but by all humanity, and surround yourself with colour and beautiful things – not necessarily expensive, but naturally resplendent. Allow yourself to blossom by wearing attractive and colourful clothes.

BRONCHITIS AND GENERAL BREATHLESSNESS (see also **asthma**)

When air enters the lungs it passes through narrow tubes called bron-chioles. In the case of bronchitis and breathlessness of an asthmatic nature the bronchioles become narrower. This can be caused by muscular contraction in the walls of the bronchioles or by mucus congestion.

∾

Your doctor can prescribe bronchodilators that will widen your bronchioles and improve your breathing. Diet is also important in the control of breathlessness and bronchitis, as the amount of mucus must be lessened. This can often be achieved by reducing dairy products and orange juice, as in certain patients oranges promote mucus activity and a better source of vitamic C for them is grapefruit which breaks down mucus, or by taking supplements of both potassium and magnesium. Potassium chloride taken as an elemental celloid (see Blackmores – Useful Addresses) will reduce the amount of mucus and the magnesium will lessen the attacks of spasm and prevent the bronchioles from narrowing.

Nutritionists agree that our diet contains almost 80 per cent less magnesium than it did in the early part of this century; hence the proliferation of illness related to spasm effects in the body. Magnesium gives elasticity, which helps counteract asthma, bronchitis, muscular stiffness, backache, sciatica and many other illnesses resulting from lack of elasticity in the cell structures.

Bronchitis sufferers have a tendency to worry about trifling little things, and an overprotective attitude to family members may lead to selfish attitudes when dealing with people outside the family. These thoughts of holding on to family, and over-protectiveness to those close to you, induce insecurity. Indifference and coldness of emotion towards those outside your own personal life lead to intellectual pride and this can manifest in absent-mindedness, with loss of nerve when dealing with the outside world.

With any respiratory illness, communication is the funda-mental element in attaining improved health. The true art in communication is listening as well as speaking your mind. Try to be more accepting of other people's views and listen to their opinions. Be more flexible. Remember, the bronchioles will go into spasm as a result of rigid thinking and restrictive actions. Tolerance and fluidity, in contrast, will bring relaxation, and the objective in dilating the bronchioles is to allow more breath to flow into your lungs.

CANCER

Uncontrolled multiplication of cells leads to the formation of tumours that may be benign or malignant. Benign tumours do not spread to other tissues; malignant or cancerous tumours do. The immune system recognises unfamiliar cells and lymphocytes help destroy them, whether they originate from a tumour or other harmful implanted material.

The key to avoiding and to treating cancer is a strong immune system. Although current medical science has not identified a single cause of cancer, it suggests that certain external factors (carcinogens) can provoke the formation of abnormal cells.

Tobacco, for example, is a factor in lung cancer, excess sun in skin cancers, and of course there is the failure of the immune system due to HIV infection which causes susceptibility to other infections. Scientists are still looking for the virus or primary exterior causative factor in cancer.

It is my view that most cancers begin on the inside from stress that disrupts the controlling electromagnetic fields that surround all living cells, including those of the immune system. Shock, trauma, fear and despondency (at both mental and emotional levels), along with environmental pollution of the air we breathe and the food we eat, are the main factors in causing cancer.

∾

There are numerous alternative and complementary therapies that can run parallel to orthodox medical treatment for cancer. After many years in complementary medicine, assisting cancer patients in dealing with the illness and the stress management of the symptoms, a number of questions have been raised in my mind. I have shared some of these with my conventional medical practitioner colleague, but as yet have received no explanation.

For example, I have questioned conventional doctors about the occurrence of cancer of the heart. I am told the incidence of this is rare – almost unknown – yet I have received no explanation. Is it that the heart is the most highly oxygenated organ in the body and cancer cells therefore cannot proliferate in a highly oxygenated environment? Or is it that the heart is a muscle and relies heavily on adequate supplies of potassium and magnesium for its action, maybe to the detriment of other organs in the body?

These two elements appear to be sadly lacking in our daily diets. In fact medical science admits that much potassium is lost in the preparation of processed foods (which most people eat) and the level of magnesium in the Western diet has dropped by 80 per cent in the last few decades.

So, who knows? Maybe a little more oxygen (the third most abundant element in the universe) and some extra potassium (seventh most abundant) and magnesium (eighth most abundant) would assist the body in fighting the cancer cells, along with the correct healing thoughts. It's a fairly inexpensive prescription!

If you have been diagnosed with cancer, do not fear the worst and do not give up hope. It is important to go on developing goals and ambitions for your life ahead. With a compromised immune system, you need to strengthen your inner creative ability and perception (whether in business or in personal relationships) in order to progress in your life.

To create additional, healthy immune cells to counteract the cells released by any malignant tumours, you must have a creative and active mind. Remember that your physical body, comprising billions of cells, listens continually to your mental demands. If you have thoughts of despair and not wishing to continue your life, your body will think the same because all its cells have a 'mind of their own' and they will act accordingly.

Be positive. You do possess some very creative and artistic traits, and you really need to work on these for the benefit of both the mental and emotional side of your life in dealing with the condition. This positive attitude will manifest in your physical cells as well as in the creation of additional immune cells to fight the illness. Participating in some form of creative art, music or craft would be of great benefit for you. This would assist in the further development of your general creativity and perception, all of which could be used for the ongoing purpose and success of your life.

It is important for you to develop willpower, not only for your own use in controlling what happens in your life, but to some degree in controlling or influencing others, either in personal or in business life. You *need to be needed* to progress in life. If you demand of your body the need to exist, tell your body in meditation (see Useful Addresses) or in visualisation, and it will respond. If the light of your personality is to shine with renewed hope, you need a physical body in which to reside. Tell your body this over and over again; it will listen.

It is also useful to cast your mind back to establish whether a major or even minor event or events occurred, maybe eighteen months or two years ago, that could be responsible for the present diagnosis. Perhaps some time in the past you were overridden in your thoughts and ideas by the strong convictions of other people? In relationships you may have been too co-operative in carrying out the requests of others, often to your own detriment and perhaps this made you feel inwardly stressed or resentful?

There are many times when we have thoughts and ideas about new projects in business, or in our personal lives, but we are reluctant to carry them out, due to lack of resolve, or we are a little timid or fearful about showing off our abilities. At times like this we really should take the initiative, and press on, as the results will astound. Because we all have inner perception and plenty of creative ideas, they just need to be released. Cancer cells are not as strong as we are encouraged to believe.

However, it is important to remember that even small numbers of rogue cells can feign normality in their behaviour and development, and by so doing they will influence other cells in the body to follow their behaviour patterns.

To enact your true purpose in life, you first have to decide which direction you want your life to take. This includes both the business side and your personal relationships with loved ones and family members; develop a positive attitude and strive towards these goals and ambitions.

Your true purpose in life will only become clear once you have taken the first step of actually doing something about it. Wilfulness and the power to act come from within you, based upon your perception of events, and how you can manipulate events. You need to be in control of your own life – both with your medical treatment and the way you run your life.

Your own optimum potential and the ability to heal yourself will only be known to you when *you take control of your own life*. Be guided by your own intuition. If this is difficult for you, just listen to the thoughts that come to you in a quiet moment in your daily life; think of those things you desire for yourself, and ask yourself how these can be manifested.

The right ideas will come to you, but remember not to brush aside the needs and desires of others just to get your own way; otherwise things will not work out for you. Take your journey one day at a time, and release the burdens and causes you have established in your own mind as to the cause of your cancer. Deposit them elsewhere; not at your home station. When you return from your visualisation on your train of thoughts or from your hospital visit you will feel renewed.

CATARRH

Catarrh is a very common and aggravating complaint brought about by inflammation of the delicate mucus membranes that line the nasal passages. It is often caused by the common cold or by an allergen such as pollen. In some cases excess mucus is produced by taking in a food or drink. This can get to the point of blocking the sinuses. Your doctor will often prescribe decongestants.

❧

Potassium and sodium-based minerals and biochemic tissue salts of Kali Mur and Kali Sulph, along with Nat Mur, are very effective against catarrh. These can all be obtained over the counter from healthfood shops.

Although allergens can be involved as a physical cause, catarrhal and chronic sinus symptoms often appear in people who continually like to impose their own ideas upon others, sometimes inadvertently rather than intentionally. These people have a feeling of 'rightness' in all they do and feel they are rarely wrong in their decision-making. They appear clumsy in their attitudes and actions, yet cover this with an air of speed and haste in getting things done.

It is important for these people to take a few steps back and try to see themselves and their actions as others may see them. The use of original ideas and the creative mind will improve the natural flow of thoughts. Interestingly, I have found that the catarrhal patient who allows change in this manner will gain more freedom of breath through the nasal passages.

CHANGE OF LIFE AND MENOPAUSAL SYMPTOMS

The change of life is a natural event that occurs in all women, normally between the ages of forty-five and fifty-five. The ovaries stop producing the female sex hormone oestrogen and the monthly periods cease. Women often use HRT (hormone replacement therapy) if they experience long-term hot flushes or mood swings. However, regular exercise and leading as normal a life as possible, with a diet that includes plenty of fresh fruit and vegetables along with calcium supplements that also contain magnesium, should help to ensure a relatively easy menopausal process.

There are many alternative and complementary therapies and products that can successfully assist the change of life, but a strong mental attitude is essential. Acceptance of change is imperative; do not think that the end of your childbearing years means a sorrowful conclusion to years of fertility. The change of life means a new beginning for a woman, as her children are normally well into their teens or young adulthood. The ones who need to make changes are the husbands and partners, as they discover that they must also adapt to the transformation in their loved ones.

The maternal role will still predominate but will mature further into a wiser, more matriarchal role; this should be promoted, along with the beginning of creative pastimes. The thoughts that harm menopausal women are thoughts of inadequacy, incompetence and fear that all their female charm and attraction is lost as physical changes also occur at this time. To counteract this, look in the mirror each day and love what you see.

The change of life is actually a new lease of life, a new beginning to be cherished. Concentrate on the positive dimension of your changing character, learn from the lessons that you experienced during childbearing days so you can impart knowledge to others. You will find that younger women will seek you out for good counsel; and, above all, love your new life.

Childhood infections

Infections in childhood are common and can be divided into specific and non-specific infections. Mumps, measles, German measles (rubella) and chickenpox are specific. Non-specific infections are coughs, colds, earache, vomiting and diarrhoea, mostly caused by viruses. Vaccines are available for most specific childhood infections.

This section on childhood infections is obviously for the benefit of parents. Always consult your doctor if in doubt about a childhood infection. The overuse of antibiotics with children has became a major problem so do not expect an antibiotic every time your child has an infection. As a naturopathic and homeopathic physician and father of five, I can safely say that none of my children was immunised against childhood infections. This was a personal decision based upon my ability to recognise and treat the symptoms of the illnesses as and when they arose.

It is my personal opinion that childhood infections stimulate the immune system and produce antibodies that will help prevent other illnesses in adult life. This view is held by many doctors of philosophy and naturopathy but I must repeat that it is a personal view, and you should consult your GP or a qualified practitioner of complementary medicine about all childhood infections.

The overuse of antibiotics lowers the immune response; this is partly why an increasing number of children are catching non-specific childhood infections. A strong immune system in children is essential and this can be attained by good diet with the use of special children's supplements and in addition some very positive attitudes to life.

Here I would like to mention a case of a child (let's call him Charles) who was continually plagued by non-specific infections, and more specifically was diagnosed as having pulmonary hypertension. Having diagnosed the causative thoughts and attitudes, I used positive thoughts in conjunction with his medical treatment to assist the healing.

After assessing the case I sent the following letter to his parents, outlining the stresses that can cause loss of elemental nutrition to the body and bring about severe symptoms:

Charles has many fine characteristics, including excellent communication skills. However, these skills will only come to the fore when he is challenged with study that stimulates his logic and creative brain. If questioned about his recent years at school he would probably indicate that he has been bored by his studies, and found the work uninteresting because his powers of discrimination are excellent and he will pick up on material he discerns as being important to him and his education.

In relationships, he requires stability and with his peers will require long-term friendship, as he will communicate well with those he can trust. He hates argument and will actually give up many things to avoid confrontation. However, he does lack the will and to a degree the courage to accept inevitable change as he develops toward puberty.

With this type of character Charles will be at peace with the world and his surroundings all the time stability rules. If, however, change is on the horizon, whether this is a friend moving away, change in communication with family members at home or a possible change of school, he will develop inner vexation and the lack of resolve to communicate his true feelings. This will not manifest as exterior or observable stress but will build as an inner tension, resulting in hypertension within the cell structures of his body.

Due to the inherent weakness of certain elements in the body, exacerbated by this inner vexation, the four elements and their metabolic processes begin to get worse. Because these elements control respiration, nerves and oxygenation in the cells, the result is pulmonary hypertension, witnessed by orthodox medicine and labelled as the cause of the symptoms, primary pulmonary hypertension. Basically this name is given to a set of symptoms, but with no known cause as far as orthodoxy is concerned.

Elemental deficiencies

The four elements concerned are phosphates: potassium phosphate, magnesium phosphate, calcium phosphate and sodium phosphate. I have mentioned the role played by the first three and would add that sodium plays a major role in calcium metabolism. If there is not a proper amount of sodium phosphate present the calcium salts cannot form new compounds to be used in the elimination processes of the lungs and the control of lactic acid and glycogen. These keep the blood in a pure state and ensure correct combustion in the cells of the connective tissue of the lungs.

Charles was typical of many children who suffer stress from being unknowingly intuitive. This gave him a sense of complacency about his studies and he was more affected by relationships due to his fear of emotional upsets. For young schoolchildren the regular rituals of home life are essential. These include eating as a family, participation with all family members in storytelling for the young, and creative play, which will not be found in front of the television.

CHRONIC FATIGUE SYNDROME OR CFS
(see also **debility**)

Chronic fatigue symptoms are variable, in that some patients will feel fatigued and uninterested in life on a daily basis, whereas others will experience highs and lows. On good days the patient will have the energy and motivation for normal life, then suddenly he or she will be unable to get out of bed the next day. Symptoms vary from exhaustion, and aches and pains in the muscles, to headaches and poor appetite with a total lack of interest in life.

❧

Orthodox medicine will treat patients on an individual basis using anti-depressants, and non-steroid anti-inflammatory drugs when pain is present. In some cases the patient experiences glandular swellings and antibiotics will be used. Alternative and complementary medicine has more to offer patients with chronic fatigue, as vitamin and mineral supplements will be of great benefit. But the practitioner must establish the exact cause of the symptoms so as to prescribe the correct minerals. The Metagenics company (see Useful Addresses) has an excellent treatment for fibromyalgia which can also be used for this condition.

The cause of CFS is often associated with feelings of inadequacy or despondency about the task set before the patient. This could be in handling relationships at an emotional level or finding their job either too demanding or not stimulating enough. Thwarted career ambitions, having been held so long in the mind of an individual, can cause symptoms of mental lethargy that transfer to the cells of the body as a lack of ability to metabolise correctly.

The way forward for chronic fatigue patients is to face the challenge of a task that may be daunting, imagine completing the task and being applauded for the end result. Visualise the end result and if this is connected with a difficult relationship it will involve completion of a cycle of events and end with reconciliation. If your work is not challenging enough, take up a hobby that utilises your skills and attain pleasure in being successful.

Students often experience CFS and this can be partly due to the unfamiliar burden of having to study, cook and generally look after themselves. A change from home life to campus life can be too much of an emotional challenge. Again, taking up a hobby or a sports activity can be helpful.

CIRCULATORY PROBLEMS

The circulatory system carries the blood around the body through arteries and veins. The blood transports oxygen and nutrients around the body and carries away the waste products for excretion by the kidneys.

∾

The efficiency of the circulation may be impaired by a weakening of the heart's action or the blood vessels may become narrow due to clogging or poor elasticity (so important for the pumping action and complete circulation of enriched blood). If your circulation is poor and you suffer cold feet or hands, or headaches are becoming a problem, your doctor can prescribe drugs to improve the symptoms. One very common cause is stress, which promotes hypertension. Another cause is lack of sufficient elastic cells in the walls of the vessels carrying the blood around the body, which reduces the circulation of life-giving blood.

Patients suffering circulatory conditions often suffer stress from the most trifling events. But to them the stress is a real problem, based upon apparently major obstacles in their lives. Patients become tense and unbending in their attitudes, even when asked to change. They can also be contradictory – something that is right today will not suit them tomorrow. The stress causes them to get agitated and they do not learn from life's experiences. They repeat mistakes over and over again, and begin to lose control.

Thoughts to heal these problems will be based upon looking

at stressful situations in a more positive manner; and realising that unfavourable events are a blessing in disguise, clearing the way for progress in life. Knowledge is gained from experience, the greatest teacher of all.

Fluidity in thinking is essential for sufferers from bad circulation. Allow yourself to act upon those thoughts that just come into your mind uninvited. They will have been sent by your intuition. Patients with circulatory problems normally govern their lives by rational thinking basing their decisions purely on logic and not on perception. You need to listen to your perceptive mind and act upon those thoughts. This will give elasticity to your thinking and to the connective tissue cells. In addition, try some mineral supplements. The Metagenics company (see Useful Addresses) have some excellent circulatory supplements but you need to consult a practitioner well versed in their products.

COLDS, COUGHS AND INFLUENZA

The common cold and associated symptoms are best treated with bed rest, warmth and the use of common cold preparations to ease the discomfort. A strong immune system is essential to overcome and prevent repetitive colds. To attain this, use vitamin C, along with Echinacea-Synergy (available from Metagenics – see Useful Addresses).

∽

Impatient, intolerant people appear to catch more colds than sedentary, quiet folk who go about life peacefully without fuss. Persistent common cold and influenza sufferers are impatient with others, always thinking they are right.

Try not to be impatient generally, and do not be dissatisfied with your attainments (irrespective of your desires in life). Rather than keep searching for new experiences, be happy with your life, and with the people around you who share your life.

Remember that both the giving and receiving of love brings strength and inner contentment which leads to calmness, patience and understanding. These attitudes will improve your immune system and prevent the recurrence of colds and flu.

Thinking that you are sure to catch a cold when you mix with those suffering the symptoms will be sure to help bring on the sniffles. And once that starts, you're convinced. Be positive when you enter a room full of people talking through their noses, and think to yourself that the vitamins and supplements you take will give you the protection you need.

I have a patient called 'Postman Pat' – she is actually called 'Post-person Pat' if I am to be politically correct. For many winter months she sneezed her way round the morning deliveries and she told me that, come October, the sea mists of Southampton would always bring on her endless winter colds.

I naturally gave her the required supplements but assured her that the cause of her colds was probably not the sea mist but the early morning chatter and exchanges in the sorting office. 'I certainly do not want other people's germs,' she remarked. And just that positive thought, of not wishing to have those germs, appears to have spared her so many colds. Whether it was the remedies or her positive thoughts I don't know, but it's worth a try if you are a regular cold sufferer. It worked for Post-person Pat!

COLIC

Colic can affect the abdomen, kidneys, ovaries and the digestive tract in general; your doctor can prescribe accordingly.

∾

As an alternative first-aid remedy for colic, the biochemic tissue salt Mag. Phos. is excellent. Use three little tablets for children, and six for adults, in a little hot water. Stir well, drink the mixture down and repeat every two hours until relief is attained. If symptoms persist after twenty-four hours seek medical advice. Colicky babies can have a couple of Mag. Phos. tissue salts placed in their milk bottles; breast-feeding mothers can take four tablets every three hours and watch their baby's grimace turn to smiles.

Colic in adults is linked to many of the emotions within, and is often linked to fear and inadequacy in making changes and decisions in life. Sometimes sufferers become suspicious about having to make rapid decisions and arrive at conclusions, because of the strong advice or demands of others. Colicky patients take too long about everything, from time spent in the bathroom in the morning to deciding what tie to wear. Continued indecision can make it tempting to choose the easy way out of situations. This attitude will affect the emotions, and will eventually lead to a major challenge, to which you cannot rise.

Change is inevitable. Accepting that change enables you to progress along your chosen path of life will improve your digestion and prevent the build-up of indecision, both mental and emotional (the main cause of colic).

CONSTIPATION

A condition characterised by abnormally infrequent and difficult evacuation of faeces. This can be accompanied by pain and loss of blood due to anal fissures and haemorrhoids.

∾

Your doctor can provide laxatives, but the best results come from a diet containing fibre, along with plenty of fresh fruit and vegetables (steamed rather than boiled and certainly not microwaved). Constipation is often ignored, and sometimes thought of as a normal part of modern-day life. But let me give a word of warning, rather than fear. Many of the cancer patients I see have a history of constipation. Bowel regularity and intestinal motility is essential for an unpolluted bloodstream.

Constipation sufferers often allow obstacles to block their paths in life; they take their eyes off the goals and ambitions they have set themselves. They are sometimes selfish in their attitudes and this can prevent progress in relationships and business. Flexibility of mind is essential for bowel motility. We must all remember that the degree to which we are successful in life corresponds directly to our degree of commitment. Obstacles will be overcome through perseverance and hard work and these attitudes to life are imperative.

To rid yourself of constipation, a harmonious balance in life is essential. Your concern about the materialistic aspects of life should not outweigh the need for spiritual understanding and belief. You do need faith on which to base your life and this will allow you to balance your material life with the more spiritual aspects that give you both wisdom and understanding of the needs of others.

When under stress you may focus on the more negative aspects of love and wisdom, instead of developing the ability to make sound decisions. (Indeed, people often become unable to make them.) It is very important for you to listen to your subconscious mind, or that inner voice that rises within you from time to time, taking care not to rationalise your thought processes to repress your intuitive or instinctive knowledge. The danger of such repression is that you could become too smart for your own good.

You should endeavour to get rid of these rigid attitudes of mind, and allow change to occur naturally, thus revealing the hidden focus that works within everyone, leading us to the real purpose of our lives. The overcoming of obstacles, the release of selfish attitudes and not always thinking you are right will bring relief from constipation.

COPD
(chronic obstructive pulmonary disease)

This is the overall name given to a number of lung conditions, including emphysema and general lung weakness caused by continual respiratory infections both as an adult and from childhood. Orthodox medicine can offer little help apart from bronchodilators and advising smokers to quit the habit.

Benefit can be obtained from taking mineral supplements and homeopathic medicine. This will improve the integrity of the mucus lining and make the connective tissue in the lung more elastic, giving better expansion. However all this must be done under the supervision of a qualified practitioner (see Useful Addresses).

Apart from environmental pollution, which will cause this condition, there is often a link with lack of personal expression. Patients are reluctant to speak their minds and frequently suffer from strong convictions and directions from other people. They can become almost subservient, even to relatives and family members. It's vital here to take control of your own life, be more in charge of your own situation and daily regime, and not be influenced to change when you are happy with things the way they are.

Patients often carry baggage or clutter from childhood inadequacies (such as being told you are not as good as your brother or sister, and they will do better in life than you). This type of baggage must be left elsewhere when you do your train journey visualisation. It's time to take on a new positive attitude of authority and command of your own affairs.

CORPULENCE AND OBESITY

An excess accumulation of fat in the body leads to obesity. However, there can also be other physical factors and it is always advisable to seek a medical opinion.

❧

Doctors will often advise diets or drugs if there are causes other than solely obsessive eating habits. This is where thought processes and changes in attitudes can counter any obsessive tendencies. Sometimes obese patients lack the ability to make sound decisions. This can lead to moral lapses and severe temptations in both personal and business life, causing feelings of inner frustration and inadequacy. These feelings lead to overeating, as the patient needs to be noticed, although the obsession is often conducted clandestinely. Where devotion to others is concerned, you do at times experience some selfish attitudes and sometimes anger, all due to your negative attitude towards love and traditional values.

Caring for your fellow man or woman brings tenderness, loyalty and respect for relationships and for life itself. People such as you need to follow a particular career or hobby, for which you have a definite inclination and for which you are talented, and you need to follow this path for a long period of time. If you persevere you will be very successful in this chosen career or path of life, and may rise to considerable heights in the business world, but in mid-life a major event will bring about a complete change of interest and career. It is also important to be creative, particularly for those not in the business world. I have an existing patient who suffers from obesity; she works for a wonderful family as a housekeeper and became very worried about her weight and her ability to continue her work adequately due to her lack of mobility.

We spoke about many things and at the consultation she remarked how she loved embroidery but always kept her work to herself, not feeling confident enough to show others. I suggested she spoke to her employer, show them the work, and ask if others might be interested. The result is a woman with more overall confidence, who is busy in her spare time with orders for embroidery, and has a sense of purpose in life.

Although this change of heart or attitude regarding yourself may appear to be the polar opposite of your previous self-image, it is of crucial importance for your personal development. When such a situation arises in your life, or if the event has already occurred and you can relate to it, intuition is of the utmost importance when deciding what action should be taken. Listening to your inner self or subconscious mind is preferable to being guided purely by intellect and reason. Do not be alarmed or worried when this event occurs, as it was almost inevitable that it would happen.

Take time to stand back and examine the challenge you face or have faced in the past, assess yourself and decide how well you have done. Give yourself more credit. Look at yourself in the mirror and love what you see. One last tip: if you are on a diet stop weighing yourself.

CRAMP

This is a painful spasmodic muscular contraction which can occur in the legs and feet whilst resting or during light sleep. It often affects the hands and fingers, due to excessive writing or typing.

❧

Doctors can prescribe analgesics and non-steroid anti-inflammatory drugs but these do not deal with the cause of the condition, which is poor elasticity of connective tissue cells. The use of mineral supplements such as magnesium will be a great help.

With severe and regular cramps, it is very important to withdraw from any restrictive practices such as being too wilful and overconfident. You also need to avoid stumbling headlong into further problems, simply because you haven't listened to others or your own thoughts. If anything, you should take things a little more slowly, possibly doing a self-appraisal, or seeking some advice from a wise counsellor, or even some quiet meditation (see Useful Addresses). In the normal noise and bustle of daily life it is often difficult to hear the 'still small voice'. Nevertheless, you should perhaps wait and listen for its guidance.

Those who refuse to do so may experience a detrimental change in their affairs or perhaps witness the collapse of their ambitions. Therefore stop, be quiet, listen, be discreet; there is a need for some silence. Those patients suffering cramps are often stretching themselves too far in life, both physically and mentally.

Another interesting aspect of some cramp sufferers is that they have a very vivid imagination, even to the point of striving to unravel the meaning of life itself. There are many aspects and events occurring in your life that tempt you to think, 'there's more to life than meets the eye'.

Use your perceptive and creative abilities to unravel day-to-day problems as they arise in the future. When meditating or taking a journey of visualisation, use your perception and intuition to bring thoughts to mind to address your current worries and problems.

CROHN'S DISEASE

This is a condition in which the walls of the gut become inflamed and thickened, and the inside becomes narrowed so food may have difficulty in passing through. The inflammation can occur at any point in the digestive system from the mouth to the lower bowel, involving just a small portion or a larger section. The cause of Crohn's disease is unknown and in orthodox medicine palliative measures are all that can be offered. Most patients live a fairly normal life, except in those cases where large sections of the gut are involved and surgery is required.

∽

Crohn's sufferers will do well to consult a practitioner in complementary medicine to assist them in a dietary approach and advise on what supplements or digestive enzymes to take for better absorption through the digestive tract. Thoughts and attitudes that aggravate and can be causative of Crohn's are often linked to emotions that are experienced through the solar plexus. Many of the emotions can be linked to fear and a sense of inadequacy about making changes and decisions in your life. This often happens with teenagers when they leave home to go to college.

Sometimes you can become suspicious and reluctant about having to make rapid decisions and arrive at conclusions, because of the demands of others. There appears to be no time to think things through and this always happens at a time when the patient has been enjoying life to the full, then suddenly one day it all changes.

Continued indecision can make it tempting to choose the easy way out of situations, even to the point of being obstinate and resentful and often making feeble excuses. This attitude will affect the emotions, and will eventually lead to a major challenge, to which you cannot rise. You need to accept that change is inevitable and will enable you to progress along the path of life.

To make future progress towards health and true happiness, you have to be willing to subject yourself to the dictates of your inner self, and the thoughts arising in your mind about the future. You are on the brink of a time of change (perhaps even as drastic as a change of career) and flexibility of mind is therefore required to adapt to whatever changes are about to occur. When the time is exactly right for the desired change to take place, you may find yourself casting aside practical and material considerations, sensing intuitively that you will take the outcome, whatever it may be, in your stride.

In the course of life we are all sometimes faced with an apparently unpleasant change but, however a change may initially appear, it is perhaps the very change we need to make in order to progress along our path of life. Non-acceptance of such a change, or the refusal to adapt to a change that has already taken place, may prove harmful in the long term.

CYSTITIS

This is the inflammation of the bladder, sometimes caused by an allergic reaction or as a complication of a bacterial infection. The patient experiences irritation or burning in the bladder, with pain in the urethra and painful urination.

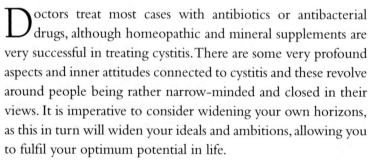

Doctors treat most cases with antibiotics or antibacterial drugs, although homeopathic and mineral supplements are very successful in treating cystitis. There are some very profound aspects and inner attitudes connected to cystitis and these revolve around people being rather narrow-minded and closed in their views. It is imperative to consider widening your own horizons, as this in turn will widen your ideals and ambitions, allowing you to fulfil your optimum potential in life.

There are of course various causes of cystitis, as in the case of a patient named Hilary (see page 19) where amalgam fillings were implicated. But, in general, you may find you have to cast aside a rigid state of mind in order to expand beyond your all-too-familiar boundaries. You need to start trusting people, and put aside your experiences at the hands of others up to now. Even a move to another town may be the expansion you require. Weigh up all the opportunities offered to you; consider them carefully, with a positive view to taking them up.

Although each opportunity in life may appear to occur at an external, material level, it also forms an integral part of your own individual evolution and destiny. Furthermore, it may offer you a chance to overcome self-doubt and reluctance to change. This, in turn, will help you trust others again, and so learn that not all help is offered for reasons of self-interest or reward. Be more fluid in your approach to life.

DEAFNESS AND WAXY EARS

Impairment of hearing can have many causes and if the condition continues you should seek professional medical advice.

Simple deafness and the overproduction of wax can be caused by a diet containing excess sugar and dairy products. However, deafness can also occur in patients who are reluctant to listen to advice, and those who repeat their mistakes. It is important to learn the lessons of life.

Sometimes your inability to learn from life's experiences may have resulted in some intense reactions to recent events, particularly of an emotional nature. Perhaps you have a sense of resignation due to previous experiences, or thwarted ambitions. If this is the case, look at the most recent events, and try to understand the lessons contained in them. Be creative and innovative, but with a sense of proportion and reality, and the current situation will soon be resolved.

It is very important for you to take a long hard look at your life and contemplate those things that appear to go wrong on a regular basis. Address the reasons why you think things do not go right for you, act upon them based upon your own thoughts, and you will prevent yourself repeating the same mistakes again and again. Concentrate and act upon the positive dimensions of your character and the qualities that people compliment you upon. In this way you can make use of all your best attributes and your whole life will take on a new dimension.

Debility, nervous and physical

A person's state of mental alertness varies throughout the day and is controlled by chemicals in the brain. Some of these are depressant (causing drowsiness) and others are stimulating (causing heightened awareness). Amphetamines are administered by doctors to increase wakefulness, but the most common home stimulants are coffee and tea.

The thoughts and attitudes that contribute to feelings of both nervous and physical debility often arise from an outlook of non-acceptance. Sometimes it is very difficult for patients to come to terms with suffering – whether it is their own, or that of those close to them, or that of the wider world – because it usually strikes them as being unwarranted, unnecessary or unjust.

When you personally feel debilitated and are directly or indirectly affected by suffering, it is little consolation to be told that it 'must be for a reason', or due to 'the forces of destiny'. Yet both these explanations hold the key to freeing you from the effects of debility.

Sometimes you can lose sight of the distinction between pity and self-pity, particularly when your emotions become involved. Viewed in a wider context, all events occur for one reason or another and it is our willingness to face these events and their consequences that leads to progress and evolution in life.

As always, suffering and difficulties can show you the way forward to renewed well-being: perhaps there are not so many accidents in life! Determination is important and should be coupled with a strong will and a powerful mind, but always used for both you and others, without thought of reward. To those people you come into contact with on a day-to-day basis, give appreciation and listen to their views, as you need to be very aware that all people are working through life to their own particular goals and ambitions.

As you adopt these attitudes, many people will call upon you for advice and opinions concerning their problems in life. Others will recognise your strength of character and determination as you become an example to those around you. Soon your debilitation will turn into boundless energy, as you see the beauty in life and your fellow human beings.

DELIRIUM AND DISORIENTATION

A confused and excited state marked by incoherence, illusions and hallucinations with confusion of thoughts and words. Normally treated with anti-psychotic drugs to modify the abnormal behaviour.

It's well worth trying some homeopathic remedies under the supervision of a qualified practitioner to help patients with behavioural disorders. However, here we must direct the thoughts of healing to the helper, as many people suffering delirium are often unaware of their erratic behaviour patterns which alternate with intervals of normal, rational thinking.

Those people who help delirious patients must get them to be more organised in their lives, and give them regular, yet simple daily responsibilities, but not of an obligatory nature that could cause them apprehension. Try to develop in the patient the inclination to label or classify things in their lives, record statements more accurately, and to place items back in exactly the correct place, as their world needs to be more tidy and orderly. However, even if patients are untidy, particularly in the home, they have an uncanny knack of knowing where everything is located.

When stress and trauma appear in their lives, deal with it very quickly, and according to your past experiences with them. Or if they have not faced a similar situation before, draw on traditional, rational methods of dealing with the problem. Be very careful not to repeat the same mistakes in handling the patient that could bring about an attack.

Try to develop a joint form of visualisation or meditation where you tell the story of the required journey of change of thought or attitude, reassuring the patient at all times. You need to develop a balance between the rational and creative mind, and between the material and philosophical world. Taking the patient to an art gallery showing modern and creative work can do this by inspiring the creative mind. Then perhaps visit a museum to see actual material or mechanical items used in everyday life. Let the patient describe what they see and feel about the items. This will bring the equilibrium essential to the left and right brain hemispheres, and strengthen their will and ambition to attain a balanced mind and a feeling of well-being.

DEPRESSION

Depression is an illness that can make you feel miserable over a long period of time, making it difficult to cope with everyday life. Women are twice as likely to experience depression as men, and 5 per cent of the general population experience these symptoms at any one time. It is treatable by your doctor with anti-depressants but this will not address the cause, which can range from trauma or stress to marriage problems, childbirth or financial difficulties. Another form of depression is SAD (seasonal affective disorder) which occurs in the winter and is best treated with light therapy and vitamins.

Complementary medicine is very effective at dealing with depression. Most practitioners will counsel the patient to establish the cause and then treat it with Bach flower essences and other natural remedies. Supplements containing vitamins A, B and C are very effective. Try not to overeat or become addicted to stimulants as a way of resolving the cause of depression.

The main cause of depression is not having the physical and mental endurance to cope with daily life. Lack of courage can fill you with so much worry or anxiety that, when you attempt to overcome it, you may become extravagant and start spending money, which you don't have, on things you really do not need. Some people develop excessive passions, maybe about some political or humanitarian issue, in order to draw their thoughts away from the deeper stress that worries them. Others who develop these obsessive tendencies can suddenly find a converse effect happening, which can manifest as weakness and immaturity.

There may be a lack of determination to fulfil your own ambitions, giving way to other people's desires instead, and possibly even becoming excessively subservient to those you perceive as being in higher authority. In cases where financial worries are at the core of the depression I have seen mature patients capitulate totally to the unreasonable dictates of a junior bank official. Depression can reduce your vigour in dealing with stress to virtually zero.

There are important thoughts and attitudes you can develop

which will soon lift your depression. Respond to these new cycles in your life, and view them as challenges you face – whether it's an emotional relationship, or a business or financial problem. Sometimes the uncertainty is actually the answer to the problem at hand. It is imperative that action of a positive nature is taken as and when opportunities present themselves. This will allow your optimum potential in life to be achieved and at the same time will restore your sense of well-being. Depression often occurs at times when opportunity appears in your life. Depressed patients view the challenge totally in the wrong manner, and do not see the need to develop their adaptability, versatility, tact and diplomacy, and display more self-confidence.

You must also be prepared to take calculated risks and to show initiative. The latter, when correctly used, can lead to success and the overcoming of known obstacles. Hesitation, and the inability to face reality, will always be eased by assessing in your own mind what the situation is showing you and what is to be learnt or gained from the challenge.

Take your journey of visualisation, think about the possible actions to be taken, and then see yourself in your mind's eye talking to the bank manager or your partner or whoever is responsible for the cause of your depression. See yourself in an ecstatic mood with the people who at the moment make you depressed.

I once had a most interesting case involving a slightly different cause of depression. The patient was a woman in her mid-fifties with everything to live for who was, even so, incredibly depressed. She had financial security, a happy marriage and devoted adult children who visited regularly, so why was she depressed? She answered my questionnaire fully, and the computer program showed that her inner personality was one of love and caring for those close to her emotionally, but also for the world at large. She also mentioned in her case history that she hated watching the evening news and many films because of the

violence perpetrated on humanity. Due to this media bombardment, she was suffering the opposite of love which is fear. This
inner fear was causing worry about all those she loved – was
something terrible going to happen to them? This was the cause
of her inner anxiety and depression.

I gave her Dr Bach's Aspen flower essence, along with some
potassium and magnesium celloids, and soon she was feeling
much better. I also made her think daily about the beautiful
things in her life and her family and realise that she could play a
part in their safety by placing a ring of golden light around them
for protection. This made her feel much happier; she had a role
to play in their lives and she felt less vulnerable.

Despondency and despair

Despondency and despair differ from depression in that depressives
make little attempt to overcome problems, whereas these patients
become despondent because their attempts at overcoming difficulties
are thwarted. Orthodox medicine will only offer anti-depressants as a
treatment, but true help will come from the patient's attitudes and
thought processes.

Patients who are unable or reluctant to broaden their outlook
or viewpoint can experience self-doubt and lack of trust in
others, choosing to manage everything themselves. This can lead
to feelings of being overburdened and then developing unfair
dealings by not including others in business or in personal affairs,
possibly resulting in legal wrangles. Similarly, a rigid mind,
unable to expand beyond familiar boundaries or territory, will
restrict the possibility of responding to new opportunities, which
– if faced – might solve the problems and form an essential part
of a patient's progress though life.

When this happens in your life, or if you have already experienced it, you will need to exercise some sound judgement. This will help you to resolve the disputes of those around you through arbitration with a capacity to see both sides of an argument. You need to have a warm heart, and to respond demonstratively to the oppressed people of the world; so give generously, both financially and in personal time, to assist with their plight. Try helping others who are worse off than yourself; some charity work will show you how the other half live and do you good as well.

Sometimes, while involved in helping others, you will hide your inner feelings, allowing your peers to think just what they please of you. Try to communicate your true feelings to those you meet in both business and personal life. You must realise there are few people in the world today who are fully aware, or conscious of their role and purpose here on earth. This is the answer for despondent and despairing people: find your role in life. When this awareness does occur and you reflect that purpose and newfound role, it will suggest to others that they are dealing with a person of very strong will and character, embodying an understanding of the needs of people, animals and the world of nature.

These people then become courageous fighters, and despite having experienced difficulties in earlier life, they will, by mid-life, be totally successful in everything to which they turn their attention. This is going to be the sole purpose in your life; you need an awareness of your role here on earth to direct you towards this understanding of purpose.

You are also a great planner, though others may tease you about always wanting a contingency plan and never rushing headlong into things without careful consideration of the outcome and its wider effects. Be the soul of discretion, going about your work peacefully and quietly without seeking applause or adulation.

Whichever path of life you are following, or even if your career is not yet fully established, profound thinking, planning and caution will always help you achieve your optimum potential. Try to excel as an arbitrator or counsellor who not only listens to all parties and their views, but also to their own conscious thoughts, before their advising fellow human beings. Advise, but never judge. These thoughts will lead you out of despair and despondency.

DIABETES

Medical treatment of diabetes is essential. Your doctor will advise you on dietary changes and most importantly about your consumption of sugar.

∽

Diabetes can arise from low-level continuous stress, but in all types of diabetes there is a need to accept that life is not governed by intellect alone. We are all faced at some time or another with an apparently unpleasant change, but however the change may initially appear, it is perhaps the change we need to make in order to progress along our path of life. Non-acceptance of such a change, or the refusal to adapt to a change that has already taken place, may prove harmful in the long term, as it places stress upon the balance between the intellect and the creative mind.

In life, the balance between intuition and logic, or the subconscious and the conscious levels of the mind, controls the fine line between harmony and discord. On the one hand, it inclines the subconscious mind to dominate logical and discriminative thinking; on the other, it can cause the repression of the intuitive powers by the intellect, resulting in a high level of left-brain activity, causing stress and worry.

Remember, if harmony turns to discord in your life, it may be a blessing in disguise. It reminds you that, if you are ignoring the deeper levels of your intuition and perception, you are doing so at your own peril.

The attitudes and thoughts required to lessen the debilitating effects of diabetes are loyalty and reverence for life and humanity. This should be paramount in your thinking. If you develop your intuitive and creative mind you will be able to use your optimum potential to assist people along their own paths of life.

Your personal insight and dedication to your fellow human beings will place you in a position where others will seek you out for advice and help. Your perceptive and intuitive mind will give confidence in taking calculated risks, which will keep you ahead of your peers in business, and give you prior knowledge and insight into any problems that may manifest within your family and amongst those close to you emotionally. Visualise and imagine yourself taking control of your own life and helping others to manage theirs.

Brian was a diabetic patient who, over the years, was becoming more dependent upon his insulin. The whole family was made so aware of Brian and his diabetes that all events revolved totally around the clock and feeding time. It was only when Brian was made aware of this fact, and that the lives of others in the family were being controlled by Brian's requirements, that he changed his attitudes and suddenly his dependency was reduced.

Never let your illness, whatever it is, become an influence that affects the lives of others to the point of resentment; it does the family and other helpers no good.

Diarrhoea and loose stools
(see also **dyspepsia**)

Watery and loose stools can be acute and may be due to something you have eaten that's upset your stomach. However, if the condition persists, consult your doctor.

◌◌

If you regularly experience this condition without a dietary connection, and there is no pathological cause according to your practitioner, there are certain remedies that will bring normality back to the digestive tract. Complete absorption of your food is essential and this can be obtained by taking a broad-spectrum enzyme supplement, along with elemental minerals.

There is too much fluidity in your thinking. You need to concentrate more, be specific on issues, make decisions and then stick to them. Do not change your mind mid-stream, so to speak. It is very important to recognise when to exercise skilful control over the volatile factors in both your personal and professional life. However, it is also important to remember that what you see as turmoil occurring in the world outside you is also, to some extent, a mirror image of what is taking place within yourself, and vice versa.

When you skilfully combine other people's talents with your own, you make progress for yourself. By the same reasoning, through carefully exercising your self-control, you will avoid the temptation merely to manipulate people and situations for your own selfish advantage. The overall answer here is to take control of your life in a systematic, businesslike and methodical manner.

DIVERTICULITIS

This is an inflammatory condition of the intestinal diverticulum. It comes about due to a tear in the muscular wall and poor mucus linings within the intestines.

～

This condition can be treated with various orthodox drugs but, to improve the passage of food through the intestines, there needs to be an efficient peristaltic action, along with a healthy lining throughout the gastro-intestinal tract. Potassium supplements, particularly potassium chloride with colloidal iron such as Blackmores Celloid PCIP (see Useful Addresses), will be of great benefit.

Patients with internal mucus problems associated with digestive disorders are often awkward types, not so much in their personality but in their control of their motor system and their extremities. If you are a sufferer try not to be too clumsy in your approach to life in general. Clumsiness will thwart the natural progression of your life, because it will result in the mishandling of potentially helpful situations. You need to exercise control and use your skills in dealing with other people's emotions. In these circumstances it is, of course, always another person or the situation itself that seems to be at fault.

It is important that you do not become intransigent in your attitudes, and, believing you have found a particular system, method or even a path of life, which is right for you, try not to impose it or your own will upon others. You do have the ability to learn new skills in addition to those you have inherited and learnt through tradition. However, you should use the skills for your own progression in life and reap the benefits for yourself and those close to you. Sometimes a career change or the expansion of an enjoyed hobby will overcome any intransigence you previously experienced in your thoughts and attitudes.

DIZZINESS AND VERTIGO

This condition can occur due to imbalances of the inner ear or of the nervous system. If the dizziness is due to a blow to the head and the condition persists, consult your doctor.

❧

Occasional dizzy feelings can be due to not listening to the good advice of others and a tendency to keep making mistakes both in your professional and personal life. There are times when we all need to listen to sound advice, whether it comes from our intuition (the inner voice) or from an outside source.

When men experience dizzy spells, they can often gain the advice they need from a woman who has the necessary wisdom. Men often succeed in life, when supported by an equally powerful woman, and if a male patient totally acknowledges the role played by his partner any dizzy spells he suffers will dissipate. Women do better by listening to their own intuition.

An effective exercise to help balance the left and right sides of the body is to visualise listening to music through one ear only, then switch to the other ear. You can do the same by looking through one eye, then the other, but it is very important to do this in a sitting position.

Dry eye

Many people are unaware that this condition exists and sufferers of mild forms of dry eye continue to experience various symptoms of redness, burning, watery and sensitivity to bright light. The condition is related to the blockage of the tiny channels that normally carry the tears and natural fluids of the eye. Your doctor can supply drops, but the best remedy is the homeopathic eye drops, Euphrasia. Surprisingly enough, there are thoughts and attitudes related to this condition.

At times you can appear impractical and changeable in the eyes of others, sometimes to the point of being contradictory. Depending upon your environment at the time, you can also switch from brilliant conversations to gloomy silences. However, having said all this, you are learning from the experiences of life, and this is leading you towards self-control in your life, and certainly more willpower to get things done.

When you begin to question the situations that are presented to you in life, rather than blindly accepting them, allow a free flow of your innate knowledge to guide you. Some contemplation and deep thinking will reveal much that has been previously hidden from you. This applies in both your personal and business life.

Allow your eyes to see more by using your intuition which will alert you to that which you have previously ignored. Try an eye exercise, such as looking at something close to you on a windowsill, then looking out of the window far away, then back to the sill, then back to a far object. This will make your eyes work harder and exercise the muscles, which in turn will stimulate the natural secretions.

DYSPEPSIA, INDIGESTION AND FLATULENCE

Dyspepsia is the name given to pain or general discomfort in the upper part of the abdomen just beneath the rib cage. This occurs soon after eating or if you have not eaten for some time. The discomfort can last a few minutes or a few hours. Your doctor can prescribe antacids; maybe you already get these from your local pharmacy. You can help yourself by eating regular meals and not too much at any one time. Do not eat late at night and avoid alcohol, coffee and aspirin.

∾

Slow down, take some time to view your role and purpose in life, and stand back from the race to make more money and create more for yourself. Do some quiet meditation (see Useful Addresses) or just spend some time thinking. It is very important to listen to that 'inner voice' and the thoughts that arise within you when you are faced with a problem or challenge, particularly of an emotional nature.

This inner voice will guide you towards the correct actions, at the right time, leading you towards the possibilities that lie in the future, and guiding you towards a fulfilling life. You have a warm heart, which will make you respond demonstratively to others, spreading love and kindness amongst your family and those in your day-to-day life. If, however, you are rushing from one crisis to the next, indigestion will follow. It is important for you to be less rigid mentally, as this will inhibit your personal development. Love of humanity, strong individuality and good judgement are all important to absorption and a healthy digestion.

ECZEMA

An inflammation of the skin which can be dry, hot, flaky and itchy, even developing blisters that may burst, causing moisture and then crusts. It can affect the whole body but frequently appears on the hands, the front of the elbows and behind the knees. It affects adults and children alike; some babies are born with eczema.

Doctors will prescribe steroid creams, emollients and other topical applications but orthodox medicine looks only at the skin for a cause, and eczema comes from within. Eczema is not infectious, so you cannot catch it or infect other people.

In my thirty years as a naturopathic medical practitioner, I have cured many cases of eczema because I treat the patient's liver. This may sound odd but eczema is a skin condition; the skin is an organ used by the body to rid itself of toxins and fatty acids in particular. Improve digestion and liver function and the eczema will disappear. You should consult a homeopath or a nutritionist for eczema treatment. Babies can be given homeopathic medicine via their mothers if being breast-fed.

In adult eczema sufferers the mind energies of truth and

accuracy play a major role in how you conduct your life, both at a personal and business level, and these energies have a profound effect upon your well-being. You should develop a strong sense of justice and precision in life, and this will leave you little time for people who fall foul of the law or just muddle along.

You are probably a person who likes order in your life. You will always replace items in their correct place, and even if others suggest you are untidy you will always know if an item has been moved. If you are not orderly then you should now try to become so, as eczema sufferers need to be organised. Knowledge and the ability to absorb information are talents of yours, and any problems that arise in your life will be best dealt with in a traditional manner, or according to a known formula. It is important to gain knowledge throughout your life.

One of my patients was little Becky, a six-year-old who had had eczema from birth. Her life had become intolerable, with weeping sores in her elbow joints and the backs of her legs, making walking very difficult. As she grew up and the time came to start school she longed to participate but her illness prevented full integration with her peers.

The illness worsened and this was about the time the family consulted me. I gave remedies for her liver, removed all dairy products from her diet, and provided large doses of elemental celloids (including potassium and calcium fluoride). Her physical condition improved by about 50 per cent but her family became a little anxious that Becky was missing infant school regularly due to the skin irritation and the stigma caused by other children seeing her scratching all day.

I was not going to change the prescription, but I did suggest some tolerance remedies for Becky, including some Dr Bach flower essences, so that she was less affected by the comments of other children, as it was so important for her to learn and take in knowledge. The parents agreed. Becky went back to school, and after six weeks she came running into my clinic ahead of her mother to show me the inner folds of her elbows and the backs of her legs. She was so proud of her new skin and the irritation was gone. She then proceeded to tell me all about school and what she could achieve. The learning process had completed the healing.

EPILEPSY

Electrical signals from the nerve cells in the brain are normally finely co-ordinated to produce smooth movements in the motor system, but these signals can become chaotic and trigger disorderly muscular activity and mental changes typical of epilepsy or seizures. Doctors will prescribe anti-convulsant drugs but these have considerable side-effects.

∾

These symptoms can be greatly eased by the use of elemental celloid minerals, due to the influence of their correct electromagnetic fields. I have already written about this in some detail (see Chapter 2). Because mind energies affect the behaviour of electromagnetic fields, it is essential for seizure sufferers to think correctly.

At times, epileptics can create the impression of holding themselves aloof from their associates and peers. This attitude is often misconstrued by others – they are really acting out their feelings of inner loneliness. If you suffer from seizures, you may have many friends and family members but still feel isolated at times. However, this comes from your insistence on being very independent. It is all very well being your own master, but you should accept help from others when they offer it.

Try not to be too hasty in your approach with others. Listen to their ideas, consider their suggestions, and then act according to your own final decision, seeing the situation through to completion.

It is essential for you to maintain a balance between your logical and creative mind. I often advise patients to create this balance by enjoying both material things and the more philosophical side of life in equal measure. For example, you could mix the latest music and movies with some mind–body reading and yoga.

FATIGUE AND ME
(see **chronic fatigue syndrome**)

FEAR (see also **anxiety**)

Fear is the opposite of love. When patients are fearful it becomes a powerful and negative energy within their physical body and affects both their mental and emotional state. Doctors usually classify fear with anxiety and apprehension.

∞

Love and understanding are very important energies within relationships, for love is much more than just an emotion or a physical attraction between two people. Understanding and wisdom enable one to learn through love, and learning how to give and receive love is one way to attain wisdom and understanding.

Fear often arises as a negative energy when people who give love and caring to the point of devotion become inwardly fearful when those they bestow their love and caring upon do not give them the same in return. It is very important for you to develop patience and to understand the needs of others in your relationships, both personal and within the broader community.

Try not to be impatient, and do not be dissatisfied with your attainments – whatever your desires in life. Rather than keep searching for new experiences, be happy with your life as it is, and with the people around you. Remember that the giving and receiving of love from others brings strength and inner contentment, which leads to calmness, patience and understanding. The overall love of life and its people overrides fear.

FEVERS

Intermittent or relapsing fevers can have many causes but mostly originate from the bites of insects, ticks and spiders and particularly infections acquired in tropical regions. Blood tests are needed to identify the culprit, so as to administer the correct treatment.

Developing an attitude of confidence and strength of character can ease chronic and periodic fevers. This will in turn strengthen the immune system to counter the invasive infection. You must learn to trust more in the actions and words of others, even if experience has shown you the negative side of others' intentions towards you at an emotional level.

Lack of trust and your own sense of self-doubt can cause you to deal with others unfairly, which may lead to a rigid state of mind that will hinder your ability to progress through life positively. Try to listen to your own subconscious mind, and spend more time considering your daily actions, and you will find – to your surprise – that your individuality and good judgement will be enhanced. Strength of character promotes a strong immune system.

FIBROIDS

*These occur in women due to the build-up of fibrous and fully devel-
oped connective tissue in the uterus. Excision is the normal procedure, but in some post-menopausal women they often atrophy.
Elemental celloids are an effective form of treatment.*

When fibrin comes out of solution fibrous tissue can develop.
It is therefore important not to appear narrow-minded in
the eyes of those around you, or uncompromising or critical in
your nature. You need to be less rigid and more flexible in your
approach to life and the way you handle situations. Sometimes
you show a lack of sympathy towards others, which can provoke
unforgiving resentment. It is vital to consider widening your own
horizons, as this will widen your ideals and ambitions, which will
in turn promote a sense of well-being and inner peace.

When faced with a panoramic view of the world and its
potential, your own adaptability will be put to the test. You may
find that you have to cast aside a rigid state of mind in order to
expand beyond your all-too-familiar boundaries to enjoy your
newfound world.

The opportunities offered at such times should be carefully
considered with a positive view to taking them up. Although
each opportunity may appear to occur at a material level, it also
forms an integral part of your own individual evolution. Women
often experience fibroids in mid-life when radical changes are
taking place – mothers find their children leaving home, and for
businesswomen this is often a time of promotion and new
responsibilities.

If your diet is lacking in potassium chloride fibroids are likely
to form, and **shedded fibrous tissue** may appear within the
menstrual blood. Do not be too alarmed, but do not allow the
condition to continue without seeking medical advice. The

shedding is perhaps the body's way of preparing for the changes that will occur to the uterine wall tissue as the monthly cycle lessens and you head towards menopause.

FIBROMYALGIA

*This is generally classified as a soft tissue musculoskeletal condition characterised by chronic musculoskeletal pain, aching, stiffness, disturbed sleep, depression and fatigue. It bears a striking resemblance to **chronic fatigue syndrome (CFS)** and **ME**, but those with fibromyalgia have more specific tenderness to the soft tissue. Orthodox treatment is rather meagre merely offering rest and non-steroid anti-inflammatory medication.*

Magnesium is the main answer, along with manganese and vitamins B6 and B1. The Metagenics company (see Useful Addresses) has an excellent treatment for this condition, which can also be used for CFS sufferers and ME.

Negative mind energy and thoughts often lead to muscular and skeletal illness. If you suffer these types of symptoms perhaps your obstinate and unbending ways cause you to miss important opportunities in life. Try to be more adaptable and diplomatic when dealing with others, and listen openly to their views. Do not be timid in your approach, but likewise do not be intimidated by other people's strong convictions.

When new opportunities, such as a different job or house move, present themselves, it is vital for you to act positively and show adaptability, versatility, tact and diplomacy. Display more self-confidence and speak your mind – say it as it is!

You must also be prepared to take calculated risks and to show initiative. When correctly used, initiative can lead to success and the overcoming of known obstacles. See yourself overcoming the obstacles and visualise taking the risks that you previously recoiled from.

The following is part of a report I sent to Haley, a patient suffering from a type of fibromyalgia:

In my type of complementary practice I feel it is important to establish, if possible, the cause of a set of symptoms, rather than treat the observable symptoms only. In your case the cause of the headache, the stomachache with nausea, along with the skin condition and the constant tiredness with muscle aches and pains, is related to two main areas. These are the digestion (and the liver in particular) and the adrenal gland function. Do not worry about these organ functions; I find no pathology. What I do find through the assessment is that both the liver and adrenal gland functions are weak, due to certain stresses that affect these two organs in particular.

Certain stresses of a particular nature (which I will expand upon) will affect the way nutrients are absorbed from your diet. A lack of specific nutrients will cause organs and endocrine glands to have poor metabolic rates, which will interfere with their perform-ance in the body. In your case potassium is lacking, along with magnesium, and this is causing the internal digestive problems and related headaches. But in particular the potassium loss is the cause of the tiredness, aches and pains and the skin condition. Eczema, although a long-term problem, is also related to the weakness of potassium in your body since you were a child. The cause of the stomachache and slight nausea is the vagus nerve, which controls the nervous actions of the stomach and is again affected by low-level, long-term stress. This you may find difficult to accept, as you appear to be very easygoing and laid-back in your personality. However, the assessment and the mineral profile I have conducted throws more light on the condition.

The computer assessment shows you to be a very caring,

understanding, logical and discriminating person with accuracy in your dealings with other people. You have a great love of colour and the beautiful things in life, both from the material and the natural world. You base your life upon traditional family values and, when faced with anxiety or worries, will use both logic and intuitive thinking to solve the problem. These are the strengths of your character and personality, but we all have weaknesses that we have to address. In your case these small weaknesses help to create the low-level inner stresses that you suffer and perhaps do not speak of to others.

Because of your caring abilities and your understanding of the needs of others, you often allow yourself to be manipulated by other people's strong convictions. You hate argument and discord and will do anything to avoid altercation. However, there are times when you feel the need to speak your mind but are disinclined to do so, as you do not wish to hurt the feelings of others. The stress you suffer comes from inner frustration due to your own willpower being overruled at times and your lack of resolve in 'saying it as it is'. You should really speak your mind and be stronger-willed about what you wish to do.

This type of inner stress causes poor potassium metabolism in the body and will lead to headaches, stomachache and the other symptoms you detail in your case history. Your adrenal glands will produce excess adrenal hormones, which the body recognises as toxic and will remove from your bloodstream by tagging the hormone with potassium molecules (yet another cause of lowered potassium levels).

My proposed treatment is a couple of months on a program of specific pharmaceutical grade supplements to correct the potassium/magnesium imbalances and a homeopathic remedy for your general constitution. The remedies and supplements are not available to the general public so I will give you the names and telephone numbers of the pharmacies concerned. You will have to mention my name as the prescribing physician.

Haley was given high doses of potassium and magnesium as Blackmores celloids (see Useful Addresses) along with B vitamins and a Metagenics product (see Useful Addresses) called Fibroplex. This contains malic acid which is so important to aid the digestion of fibromyalgia sufferers. Three months of treatment have seen Haley make a full recovery and she is now taking a maintenance dose of the remedies on a daily basis.

FLUSHING (see **fevers** and **change of life**)

GALLSTONES

A calculus or calcification, formed as a 'stone' in the gall bladder or bile duct. Often requires removal, as the pain is intense.

∿

Gallstones are often linked to pent-up anger and unresolved resentment because the obstacles in life have proved too great to handle. It is now very important that you take a long hard look at your life. Consider why things just do not seem to go right for you, act upon them based upon your own thoughts, and you will prevent the same mistakes from repeating themselves again and again. Concentrate and act upon the positive answers and ideas that arise in response to your questions.

GLANDULAR FEVER

Intense but intermittent tiredness, temperature and general feelings of lack of interest and lassitude, with swollen glands and tonsils. Often treated with antibiotics and rest.

∿

These symptoms frequently occur at a time of intense study and long hours of mental concentration, accompanied by a lack of regular meals. Vitamin and mineral supplements are essential for hard-working students.

When you begin to question the situations that are presented to you in life (particularly when faced with large amounts of mental study or exertion), allow yourself time to think ahead and consider what results you will obtain for the effort. Some contemplation and deep thinking will reveal much that has been previously hidden from you and that you had not imagined possible, in both your personal and business life. During this period there will be times when you suffer 'inner loneliness', but the contemplation will bring you freedom from any restrictive practices that govern your life at present, and comfort can be obtained through some religious or spiritual activities. Sometimes this state of loneliness may manifest with symptoms of mental or emotional anguish. If this occurs, counselling may help to re-establish some equilibrium in your life.

GLAUCOMA

This is the name given to a group of conditions in which the pressure in the eye builds up to an abnormally high level. This compresses the blood vessels in the eye and may lead to irreversible nerve damage with permanent loss of vision. This condition is serious and needs professional medical intervention. Natural remedies will help lessen the pressure behind the eye and should bring partial relief.

∽

Eye conditions such as glaucoma and cataracts may arise from thoughts and attitudes of 'turning a blind eye', so to speak, to immoral or distasteful happenings in one's life, perhaps from many years back. Or perhaps you do not respond to things plainly put before you, ignoring the issue at hand and taking another route or an easier way out of the situation.

It is very important to see and observe, and respond to the flashes of insight that can resolve the current problems in your life. Action at the correct and crucial moment is paramount. Listening to your intuition, or inner voice, will provide the answers to the decisions you have to make, particularly those of an emotional nature.

Contrary to what your logical mind might tell you, in order to arrive at the correct decision, you should use intuition rather than intellect, and inspiration rather than reason. Patience and caution can safeguard you from impetuosity, which is sometimes mistakenly taken for inspired spontaneity. High moral standards are required for you to progress successfully on your path of life. You need integrity and maturity to keep you from making those decisions that will divert you from your true purpose. You have to see things in a true and relative way, and observe with clarity what you are being shown.

If you are a sufferer from glaucoma, visualise the clarity in life as you saw it before your eyesight was impaired and look towards that rising dawn of enlightenment. Clarity of mind may help prevent any further damage to your eyes.

GOUT

Gout is a disorder that arises when the blood contains increased levels of uric acid, a by-product of the metabolism excreted in the urine. When the concentration in the blood is excessive, uric acid crystals may form in various parts of the body, but especially in the foot and big toe joint.

Dietary changes and less alcohol will prevent the excess formation of uric acid, along with biochemic tissue salts (which your homeopathic practitioner can prescribe) – see Useful Addresses.

If you suffer gout, you need to take stock of both your destiny and the path of life you see yourself on at present, and to review any new beginnings or cycles of events that are looming on the horizon. So far in your life, when destiny has taken a hand it has appeared as though the events which happen to you are unaffected by any influence you may attempt to exert over them. And, by the same token, your problems seem to solve themselves. This is why you are inclined to take a happy-go-lucky view and assume that fate will solve all worries for you, but this will not always be the case.

This is why you must realise that, in life, you reap that which you sow, always benefiting from good deeds you have carried out in the past. If you eat too much your digestion will suffer; if you drink too much your big toe will suffer. However, where destiny is concerned, only the passage of time reveals the true course of events.

If you can develop a strength of character that includes considerable determination, particularly when getting things done, at both a personal and business level, you will be able to exercise more control over your own destiny. It is important for you to have a strong will, but not to the point of enforcing your will upon others.

Try not to be self-opinionated or over-indulge in those things you enjoy – just a wee drink now and then will be permissible. Ask your practitioner about sodium salts for gout.

GRIEF

An emotion suffered after bereavement or a loss that can be either personal or material.

The types of people who suffer long-term grief are normally those where mental and emotional stability is of paramount importance to their way of life. These people hate argument and acrimony and will do much to avoid confrontation. If you are grieving now you will probably hide your inner feelings from others. This is all very well, but for those you care for emotionally and still share your life with, it is important to show your true feelings. Harmony and balance of the emotions is important, and the linking of emotion with mental stability will instil a depth of feeling to be shared by all those around you. Tell people how you feel. If you have lost a loved one it's time now to celebrate their life and enjoy your memories of the past time you spent with them here on earth.

Your caring attitudes to those around you, and the manner in which you display your care for the oppressed people of the world, will endear you to many people, which in turn will tempt others in places of authority to call upon your services. This may be in the form of counselling others facing grief and bereavement, as the greatest teachers are those who have experienced the events themselves. These thoughts and directions will turn your grief to feelings of happiness and the acceptance of life's cycles.

HAEMORRHOIDS

Commonly known as piles, these are enlarged blood vessels – either inside or outside your back passage. The blood vessels become enlarged when subjected to pressure, for example when straining with constipation or during childbirth.

The use of a homeopathic ointment called Hamamelis is very effective and this is available in most health shops. Apply after bathing and after stool. Attitudes and thoughts to develop are similar to those listed under **constipation** (see page 123). These include flexibility and bending to the ideas and thoughts of others, rather than being headstrong.

Try to develop as many special virtues as you can, but particularly your left-brain consciousness which controls both logic and discriminative thinking. This will give you sharpness of thought and a quick wit, along with an added sense of humour. Rarely will you make the same mistake twice, as you will learn well from the lessons of life, and this will lead you to become a person displaying both kindness and affection.

A hairdresser I saw some time ago suffered haemorrhoids, a common complaint for people who stand for long hours each day. It turned out that she was a little unbending in her attitudes towards the staff in the shop. (This I established when one of the staff actually consulted me on another matter.) I supplied remedies for the circulation and supplements to provide more elasticity. However, the condition only really improved when many of her staff resigned and she had to face the real reason why she could not keep her stylists.

Once the reason was addressed and her attitudes changed towards others, the remedies and supplements began to take effect and the haemorrhoids shrank.

HAYFEVER (allergic rhinitis)

Antihistamines are used for hayfever, which is suffered by nearly three million people each summer. The condition involves inflammation of the nose and upper airways, resulting from allergic reactions to pollen, dust, animal fur and house dust mites. It is best treated by natural remedies to improve the quality of the mucus linings. If these are in good order they will deal adequately with the dust and pollen without causing a reaction.

∽

A llergic reaction and inflammation occur when the airways are dry and the mucus integrity is poor, often partly due to a lack of fluidity in the patient's thinking. The patient is usually rather set in their ways and not inclined to alter their opinions even when asked to change.

As a person suffering allergic reactions, both your personal and business life appears to be conducted in a very precise manner, and you impress people by your accuracy and fair judgements. You do have a tendency to label and classify things, as you like your world to be correct and orderly, and you have little time for those who just 'muddle along' without direction. You are sometimes inclined to be impatient and need to exercise more control over your initial reactions to people who question your motives. You do have some very profound thoughts and ideas, normally based upon a traditional framework, coupled with strong family values.

There are times when you feel lonely but you dislike talking to others about your inner feelings. Try to be more communicative and less rigid in your approach to life.

Farmer Solomon was such a case. He consulted me year after year at harvest time suffering acute hayfever and coryza; the various remedies I supplied helped to relieve but certainly did not cure the condition. One year I spoke in depth about his mental and emotional outlook on life and realised that here was a man with very strict rules on how he conducted his life and who expected others to be similar. I mentioned that we are all different, we deal with stress differently and should rely more on communication with our fellow human beings to make the world go around more smoothly.

Solomon disliked change, detested some of the developments taking place in farming (thanks to EC rules and regulations), and preferred the way things were when his father ran the farm before him. This harvest time Solomon called one evening to say that the remedies appeared to have worked this year. He admitted to me that he had now resigned himself to the inevitable changes in his farming life and he communicated more with the Ministry and his staff. Mentally and emotionally, he sounded less stressed. The seeds of thought I had planted did well on the Solomon farm.

HEADACHES (see **migraines**)

HEART CONDITIONS (see also **angina, circulatory problems** and **blood pressure**)

Being a vital organ, the heart requires elasticity for its pumping action and can be affected adversely by many factors including stress and incorrect diet, leading to fatty deposits and narrowing of the blood vessels.

Stress is more likely to be responsible for blood pressure and angina. Around 1 per cent of the population suffer some form of heart-related illness in the UK.

∾

The main influence affecting the performance and general health of the heart is stress, and the burden placed upon this vital organ by worry. The heart is an organ related to love and I do not mean this in a 'hearts and roses' fashion, but in respect of the emotion which is the opposite of love – fear. It is fear which triggers lack of elasticity in the heart, causing spasms in particular. As the heart and the general circulation play an important part in everyone's well-being I am going to include here some general text as a guide for anyone suffering heart conditions, but also as a guide to maintaining a healthy heart.

The world today is marked by a tendency towards emotional display and emotional disorder. That is why, in this day and age, love is linked to relationships, and our understanding of one another in relationships is always linked to love. In this context, love becomes more than just an emotional or physical attraction to another person. Understanding enables one to learn through love, and learning how to give, and at the same time receive, love is one way to develop meaningful relationships.

You must endeavour to become a person with certain ideals; and in your relationships, both personal and business, you should display calmness and a general strength of character, with honesty. This honesty will show through to those you choose to share your life with, and your example will enhance the lives of those people you are close to emotionally.

Patience and kindness are part of your understanding, particularly of the needs of others, and your love of humanity as a whole makes you a person of truth and integrity. When considering the attributes of love, patience, and the understanding of others' needs, it is very important that during your lifetime you also receive from those close to you the same love and understanding in return. If this is not forthcoming, it can manifest as inner frustration and even resentment, not only towards those close to you, but to humanity in general, particularly those with substantial financial assets, turning itself into jealousy. This frustration and resentment will cause the heart to become less elastic and begin to spasm.

A further asset to develop in your personality is tact and foresight. Try to develop good diplomatic skills in handling people and be conscious of their needs. Another aspect of the mental and emotional stresses that can affect the heart is that some types of people are rarely satisfied, even with their highest attainments. Aim to do well in all you undertake, and, given support from an understanding partner or business colleague, you can reach the top in your chosen career.

The above character traits will support you well through life, and, if used to the full, will provide ample opportunity for you to reach your optimum potential. However, if during your life you experience unavoidable stress or trauma, the above-mentioned

qualities may manifest as fears and anxieties, coupled with coldness and indifference to those you love best. To overcome these
particular problems, you need to concentrate on your inner
qualities to bring the peace and harmony back into your life.
Love, peace and harmony, along with understanding of the needs
of others, will safeguard against heart disease.

HEARTBURN, ACIDITY AND GENERAL INDIGESTION

*Indigestion occurs when the acidic digestive juices flow back (reflux)
from the stomach to the oesophagus (the tube your food goes down to
reach your stomach) and further into the throat, causing very
unpleasant effects in the mouth.*

∽

There are many simple remedies for indigestion, but it is best
to consult a practitioner in natural medicine to advise you
on diet, supplements and digestive aids. Because so many people
suffer digestive disorders I am going to make some overall
comments about attitudes and thoughts that will aid digestion in
general, as so many patients I have seen over the years experience
their emotions through the solar plexus and the related organs of
digestion.

Harmonious balance in life is essential for us all, and this is
especially true regarding the material and the spiritual dimensions of life, where our concern for the materialistic aspects of
life should not outweigh the need for spiritual understanding
and belief.

We all need faith on which to base our lives, and this allows us
to balance our material life with the more spiritual aspect which
gives both wisdom and understanding of the needs of others.
When under stress you may develop digestive disturbances. This

is to do with the more negative aspects of love and wisdom. Instead of developing the ability to make sound decisions, you often do the complete opposite (developing the inability to make them).

It is very important for you to listen to your subconscious mind, or that inner voice that rises within you from time to time, taking care not to repress the intuitive or instinctive knowledge with rational thoughts. The danger of such repression is that we can become too 'clever' for our own good. You should aspire to get rid of rigid attitudes of mind, and allow change to occur naturally, thus revealing the hidden focus that works within all people, leading them to the real purpose of their lives.

If you do suffer continual digestive problems, even after periods of medical treatment, it may mean that you have not yet realised your optimum potential in the area of devotion to your fellow man or woman and to life in general. You must continue to be single-minded and purposeful, and be loyal to those close to you in both personal and business relationships. Try to avoid anger when things do not go the way you thought they would. Events often occur for a reason, sometimes to show the way forward, perhaps in a direction you had not previously thought possible. Listen to those thoughts that arise in your mind when in a quiet mood and use them for a new direction in life.

HEAVY PERIODS

Five per cent of women see their doctors about heavy periods. If you also pass clots you should ask your doctor for further advice. Most women experience cramping with heavy periods and this can be helped with mineral supplements.

The following thoughts and attitudes can be associated with heavy periods. Do you sometimes find you act in a clumsy manner, not only physically, but also in the handling of your own affairs and your relationships with others? Such clumsiness may thwart your natural progression through life because it can result in the mishandling of potentially helpful situations.

In these circumstances it is, of course, always seen as another person or the situation itself that is at fault. A similar intransigence is found in those people who, believing they have found a particular system, method or path of life, be it material or even religious, which is right for them; also become convinced that it is right for everybody else.

If the above statement rings true, then you need to take action to bring about some changes, enabling you to attain your optimum potential and well-being. Normally you will have an innate thirst for knowledge and a need to know the reasons behind everything; this is matched with a keen and profound intellect. However, when under stress, there is a tendency to be a little narrow-minded and critical. Ideas should proliferate when you are faced with a challenge in both personal and business life. Although these ideas will be fresh and creative, they will always be presented within a traditional framework. This background to your way of thinking is mostly based upon your education or upbringing.

The predominant attitude for you should be of correctness in all things, but you can be uncompromising when asked to change your original thoughts or plans. Your personal and business affairs should contain accurate statements, along with a strong sense of morality and justice towards those you mix with.

You need to be a little more organised; develop the inclination to label or classify things in your life, record statements more accurately, and put items back in exactly the correct place, as your world needs to be more orderly.

HERNIAS

A condition where an organ or part of an organ protrudes through structures normally containing it. Medical advice should be sought if you think you may have a hernia.

∾

Hernias (including hiatus hernias) normally occur due to straining a part of the body. Poor elasticity of the connective tissue causes a tear that fails to heal, allowing the continual protrusion. Many conditions arising in the body emanate from elastic tissue cells being in poor condition. To me this indicates that many people today are far too rigid, self-centred and egotistical in the way they deal with other people.

Flexibility of mind is required for hernia sufferers and this means that you must expand your ability in adapting to changing circumstances. You will find that listening to the guidance of others, as well as listening to your own inner thoughts or intuition, will enhance your general powers of communication and flexibility of mind. As you achieve this goal, your powers of observation, and your growing concern for the deeper aspects of life, will teach you that everything happens for a reason, and worrying will change nothing. Remember that communication requires listening as well as speaking.

HYPERTENSION
(see also **blood pressure, high**)

I would like to offer a few more thoughts about the control of hypertension. It is very important to understand that in order to enact your true purpose in life you will have to create it. Decide which direction you want your life to take (both in business and personal relationships), develop a positive attitude and strive towards these goals and ambitions. Lack of direction, and the stresses associated with it, cause tension to build up.

Your true purpose in life will only begin to become clear once you have taken the first step to actually doing something about it. A strong will and the power to act come from within you, based upon your perception of events, and how you can manipulate these events. Playing a waiting game or relying on others for advice or even a financial handout is not the answer.

HYPOGLYCAEMIA
(see **blood pressure, low**)

HYSTERICAL OUTBURSTS

This is known as a psychoneurosis condition with symptoms of lack of control over acts and emotions exacerbated by anxiety, self-consciousness and exaggeration of sensations experienced. These symptoms require careful monitoring and treatment by a doctor.

Many incorrect thoughts and attitudes (especially long-term feelings of inadequacy and inferiority complexes) can bring about the symptoms of hysteria. The way forward for these sufferers is to develop willpower, not only for their own use in controlling what happens in their lives, but to some degree in controlling others (whether in personal or in business life). Hysteria often arises as a result of others creating avoidable situations in which nobody else intervened to prevent mishap.

Hysterical people are sometimes overridden in their thoughts and ideas by the strong convictions of others. In relationships they may be excessively co-operative in carrying out the requests of others, often to their own detriment, causing themselves to experience resentment and frustration.

These people often have thoughts and ideas about new projects in business, or in their personal lives, but are reluctant to expedite them due to their lack of resolve, or being a little timid or fearful about showing off their abilities. At times like this, one really should take the initiative, and press on, as the results will be astounding. Most people who suffer hysterical outbursts do have inner perception and plenty of creative ability; it just needs to be released in a different manner.

IMPOTENCE

A condition often caused by a combination of physical and psychological factors, best treated by an initial discussion with your doctor who will direct you towards counselling or establish whether a physical problem exists.

❦

As impotence occurs later in life for men, there are certain attitudes and thought processes that can help the condition. The mature man must recognise the need for continuing attitudes of courage and vigour to take risks and accept challenges in the material world; this will provide the opportunity to put your long-term plans into action. As men age, they often slip back into a 'comfort zone' (not only within the relationship with their partners but also in the workplace), thinking that enough exertion is enough and perhaps retirement is just around the corner.

The ability to achieve genuine success in the material world, at any age, also stems from your own state of personal harmony, the attainment of which requires you to overcome immoral tendencies or affairs of the heart and reconcile yourself with your enemies. This latter comment can either be related to outside events or to the unruly elements that exist within you at present, which can also develop from discontent within a partnership. However, seeking gratification or enjoyment elsewhere can actually lead to impotence, as the unruly events within will reflect in the emotional dimension of your life.

Real opportunities for harmony always contain an element of hard work and commitment, for which strong nerves and moral courage are essential. Your own conscious input of these two qualities will ensure the success of your current projects, and the resolving of any personal problems such as impotence.

INSOMNIA

Difficulty in getting to sleep or staying asleep can have many causes, often associated with worry, anxiety or depression. Doctors will prescribe sleeping tablets or give additional drugs for the mental worries.

∾

If you experience disturbed sleep and you lie awake at night worrying about the day just gone, or the day to come, or you are concerned about family members and the way they are leading their lives, you need to examine your current philosophy and view of life.

The question has to be asked: Are you leading your own life in a manner that is conducive to your own personality? And are you accepting that all people, even close family, are living their own lives to the best of their ability? Maybe you should step back and look at past events and your relations with your fellow human beings, and consider whether they were how you would wish them to be. If not, then you should spend some quiet moments thinking about inner qualities of caring, perception and tolerance. Work on these aspects with some quiet thoughts on constructive attitudes at night, rather than worry and consternation. The worries that disturb your sleep will turn into peaceful thoughts if you look at your own role in events and not the wrongdoings of others.

IRRITABLE BOWEL SYNDROME (IBS)

This is one of the most common conditions of the gastro-intestinal tract and affects one-in-five of the population of the UK. Symptoms can vary from cramps (mostly in the left-hand side of the abdomen) to sharp pain that is eased by passing wind or a motion. The abdomen can become bloated and painful and you may experience constipation or loose motions.

∾

Over the years I have treated many patients with IBS using many different types of complementary therapies, in some cases referring to other practitioners, and in all cases reducing stress. Because the material world we live in brings both mental and emotional worries from relationships and business concerns, the priority is to address the IBS patient's stress.

A case that comes to mind involved a woman who I never saw at my clinic as she lived many miles away. We therefore dealt with the case by letter and fax. Here is an extract from the case report:

In your case the cause of the irritable bowel syndrome and the bad skin appears to be twofold. The skin condition is related to the performance of the liver and its ability to process fatty acids from your diet. This is not a worrying pathological condition; it is just that your liver is sluggish or torpid, as we would describe it in naturopathic medicine.

The second factor is stress-related, causing the IBS. It's not that you experience severe environmental-type stresses, but you do have inner worries and anxieties that affect the solar plexus and in turn the liver, as this organ is always affected adversely by stresses of the stomach.

Let me begin with the stress or inner anxieties that I believe you suffer. I see from your completed case notes (which information I have put through my computer program) that you are an auditor which involves an accurate, methodical and logistical approach to your work. This will bring with it some stress.

These characteristics are fine but when completing the assessment on you I find you have many other attributes, including perception and creativity. This will naturally bring you some inner stresses, as you will have to conduct your working life based upon known procedures and practices, whereas often you would like to use more creative and perceptive thinking. Your ideas often abound with possible changes, but perhaps you cannot implement them and this will cause the types of stresses or inner anxieties I am speaking of.

There are times when you would like to suggest changes in procedures but are reluctant to do so. This type of thinking will also reflect in your personal life. There may be times when you would like to say more about a subject or your emotions but decide to keep quiet when you really should be venting your feelings.

In naturopathic medicine we are well aware of what type of stress will affect which area of the body, and the resulting symptoms. In your case it is the performance of the liver, as I have previously mentioned. However, there are things we can do. I would like to suggest remedies for the stomach, which in turn will heal the liver and subsequently the skin, and will lift the depression you experience. I will also help you to cope with stressful times by giving you tolerance remedies that will hopefully cure the IBS. You mention in your case history the preparation for children; here I can make suggestions for your husband with certain amino acids to improve sperm count and general motility.

Irritable bowel syndrome sufferers will experience many events during their lives that cause radical changes, sometimes considered unwelcome at the time. Yet these events will clear the way forward, showing you the direction of your real purpose in life after the period of inner conflict. This inner conflict may be a personal or business worry, but the overcoming and the emergence from conflict – whether experienced within oneself or externally with others – coincides with the removal of outdated or superfluous aspects of your life. This will allow an unhindered move forward into the future. Changing your job, friends or house are all ways of moving forward in life.

This move forward, or change from your normal routine, needs to come alongside the realisation that your highest attainment in the control of your own mental and emotional states will be gained through life experience, the greatest teacher of all.

Changes in your life will often occur as the result of another's actions, and you may often think to yourself that the stress or trauma emanating from the change was none of your own doing. This will promote inner resentment, but do not dwell on this aspect; it will do you more harm than good, particularly in terms of your own health and well-being.

Kidney and Adrenal Gland Problems

Uric acid is removed from the blood by the kidneys. Lying on the upper part of the kidneys are the adrenal glands which produce a number of important hormones called corticosteroids. These natural hormones reduce inflammation in the body after injury and stress. Conversely, induced stress will affect the function of the kidneys and adrenal glands.

∾

L ow levels of stress will allow a natural flow of life energy through the body. However, if stress builds up in the body, causing congestion of this energy flow, the blockages will affect the function of kidneys and the urine flow, as well as the adrenal gland function.

Kidney disease (apart from that inherited genetically), along with adrenal gland malfunction, is related to excess or, conversely, lack of willpower. If you suffer the symptoms I have described there is a continual need for both will and power in your personality which, if handled correctly, can arise from your own strength of character, but must not be used in a selfish manner. We all have an innate physical fight or flight mechanism. At a mental and emotional level you need to develop perseverance, particularly when faced with a challenge of one kind or another. This is a trait that needs to be worked upon to obtain a higher degree of self-confidence in your personality.

Your type of personality requires a challenge in order to respond actively on a daily basis, but these have to be positive challenges and not negative or possibly immoral projects that could fall foul of the law. The ability to respond to a personal challenge will lead you to rely upon yourself rather than others to overcome the obstacles you encounter along life's path. Do not be easily led by other people's strong convictions; have a mind of your own and stick to the decisions you make.

Your material success and financial security will only be attained through your own hard work and determination, and not through inheritance or another similarly easy way. You will have to work for everything you desire, whether at a personal or business level. It is very important that everything is done decently and in order. You need to become a person who works according to rule, morals and precedent, in both your personal and business life.

As you aspire to the above qualities, it is very important to remember that others also have their rights and needs; and that which is exactly right for you, may not be right for them. There must be a realisation that others around you, who adhere to beliefs and codes of behaviour that differ from your own, are, in fact, progressing along their own chosen path in life, and we must all learn to respect this.

Lᴇᴛʜᴀʀɢʏ

Feelings of tiredness and lethargy, with little or no interest in your current lifestyle, job or relationships, often stem from a lack of general direction and a sense that you have no purpose in life.

Purpose and determination are inter-linked; with no direction, there is little need for resolve. I mentioned in Part One of this book that cells within the body have a role and purpose. If this is lacking in the patient's personality, it is a distinct possibility that the body will develop illness due to lethargy (a clear case of the mind–body connection).

Your inability to learn from life's experiences may sometimes have resulted in intense reactions to recent events. Perhaps you have a sense of resignation, due to previous experiences, or thwarted ambitions or a traumatic relationship. If this is the case, look at the most recent events, and try to understand the lessons contained in them. Be creative and innovative, but with a sense of proportion and reality, and the current situation will soon be resolved. It's all to do with learning the lessons of life, so contemplate the recent message life handed you and don't make the same mistake again.

If you still feel lethargic after a few days, take a look outside, a walk in the park or the countryside, and view nature's creatures and the beauty of a landscape or seascape. I have often told lethargic patients to set their alarm clocks and get up early to view the dawn and the beginning of a new day.

LEUKAEMIA (see **cancer**)

ME (see **chronic fatigue syndrome** and **fibromyalgia**)

MENIÈRE'S SYNDROME

This is a disorder in which excess fluid builds up in the inner ear, causing vertigo, noises in the ear and gradual deafness. It is normally treated with an antihistamine, and sometimes an anti-anxiety drug, along with diuretics to reduce the fluid in the inner ear.

I have had many Menière's patients attend my clinics. In addition to elemental minerals to balance the fluids in the body, and homeopathic remedies noted for their success in treating this condition, I have referred patients to a holistic dentist (see Useful Addresses). The leakage of mercury from amalgam fillings or the toxins from root canals are often the physical causes of Menière's syndrome. If the condition is related more to the imbalance of fluids in the ear, certain thought processes and attitudes can help to reduce the symptoms.

Fluid balance relies upon the correct proportions of both sodium and potassium in the body fluids. To attain and maintain this equilibrium, it is imperative to consider widening your own horizons, not viewing one direction or goal in isolation. A broader view of your life's direction will in turn widen your ideals and ambitions, which will bring balance to your life.

When faced with a panoramic view of the world and its potential in which you can participate, your own adaptability is put to the test, and you may find you have to cast aside a rigid state of mind in order to expand beyond your all-too-familiar boundaries.

The opportunities offered at such times should be carefully considered, with a positive view to taking them up. Although each opportunity may appear to occur at a material level, it also forms an integral part of your own individual evolution. Furthermore, perhaps it is your opportunity to overcome your self-doubt and reluctance to change, and will in turn give you the opportunity to trust other people again.

MENOPAUSE (see **change of life**)

MENSTRUAL PROBLEMS (see **fibroids**, **heavy periods** and **premenstrual syndrome**)

MIGRAINES AND HEADACHES

Migraine is a severe condition consisting of head pain combined with other symptoms such as nausea and vomiting, along with visual auras that sometimes warn of an oncoming attack. These severe migraines can be triggered by hormonal changes, excess coffee, wine or dairy products, but mostly by stress, anxiety and worry.

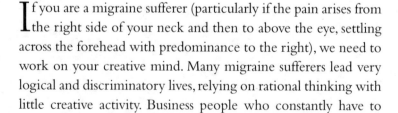

If you are a migraine sufferer (particularly if the pain arises from the right side of your neck and then to above the eye, settling across the forehead with predominance to the right), we need to work on your creative mind. Many migraine sufferers lead very logical and discriminatory lives, relying on rational thinking with little creative activity. Business people who constantly have to work within the parameters of rationalism suffer right-sided headaches, as all the thinking processes are directed to the left brain. However, the overall treatment for both left- and right-sided head pain is balanced thinking.

Your creative ability and perception is an area within your general character that really needs to be developed for the progression of your life, whether this is to do with business or personal relationships. Everyone has some creative and artistic traits, and these really should be worked upon. Participating in some form of creative art, music or craft would be of great benefit. It would assist in the further development of your general creativity and perception, all of which could be used for the ongoing purpose and success of your life.

It is important for you to develop willpower, not only to control what happens in your life, but to some degree to control others, either in personal or business life. It sometimes happens that you are overridden in your thoughts and ideas by the strong convictions of other people, and in relationships you are exces-sively co-operative in carrying out the requests of others, often to your own detriment. There are many times when you have thoughts and ideas about new projects in business, or in your own personal life, but are reluctant to expedite them, due to your lack of resolve, or being fearful about showing off your abilities.

At times like this you should definitely take the initiative, and press on, as the results will astound you. You really do have inner perception and plenty of creative ability; it just needs to be released.

I would like to mention here an interesting case of a woman of forty-five who had severe migraines which she had suffered for more than ten years. The case was cured very quickly with a combination of homeopathic remedies and some Blackmores celloids (see Useful Addresses). There was no need to implant any thoughts about control of emotions or mental attitudes. Mary went away delighted and mentioned on her way out that she would send her husband along who had suffered sciatica and backache for years. This is the more interesting part of the case study.

Sure enough, George arrived one day with the opening comment: 'My wife says you can cure my sciatica.' This statement struck a chord immediately. Here was a patient with an attitude of 'my wife says' or, perhaps, 'there is no way I am going to do what my wife says . . .'

I treated George with every remedy in the book. I even chatted about stress and worries, and 'no worries in my life doc' was the answer. George would not respond and we parted company. Some months later Mary appeared with some back-ache and muscle spasms due to doing too much work in the garden. I asked why George did not participate in the digging and gardening in general. 'Oh no,' said Mary, 'he can't do that sort of work because of his sciatica and bad back. When he comes home from work he has to have his meal waiting for him, slip-pers in position by his chair and the TV remote at the ready.'

There was no way George wanted to be cured of his bad back and sciatica when he had a partner like Mary to do all the work. But I am afraid that George will one day reap the rewards of his resistance to change.

MYALGIA (see **fibromyalgia**)

NEURALGIA

This refers to pain in a nerve and one of the most common is trigem-inal, affecting the face, neck and head. Neuralgia can also be experi-enced in the breast and ovaries, and children often suffer stomach neuralgia. For children's problems try the tissue salt of Mag. Phos. in warm water, twice a day before meals.

Pain relief in neuralgia is often difficult to achieve, as painkillers do not address the cause, which may be trauma to the nerve or poor nourishment of the nervous system in general. This can be achieved by the use of the minerals potassium and magnesium, which are the main constituents of nerve fibre.

If you have to endure neuralgia it may be that your obstinate and singular thoughts sometimes cause you to miss important opportunities in life. Try to be more adaptable, diplomatic and versatile (especially when dealing with others, and listen openly to their views and opinions). Do not be timid in your approach, and likewise do not be intimidated by other people's strong convictions.

OBSESSIONS

Obsessions occur when people's mental attention focuses on one singular event or activity, which can be either positive or negative.

People often enjoy their obsessions and this is not a problem if it does not interfere with the lives of others. Obsession becomes a hazard when it begins to infiltrate into life to the detriment of all other activity, causing mental or emotional health problems. If this occurs counselling is essential.

Many obsessions, such as the continual washing of hands, or the over-concern with pristine cleanliness of oneself or one's household, stem from guilt or remorse at a subconscious level. Patients such as these need help to erase the cause, which may come from past experiences of abuse at the hands of another, either physical or mental. Obsessions in general appear to have a deeper cause and this must be discovered and dealt with by the patient.

OSTEOARTHRITIS

This is the most common type of arthritis which affects the cartilage or coating that covers the ends of bones, causing roughness and thinning. Fluid collects and causes the swelling of the joint. Doctors have no answer to osteoarthritis, putting it down to age and wear and tear, yet it affects five million people in the UK alone. They can prescribe drugs for the pain and stiffness, but the only answer for the chronically affected is to replace the joint.

∼

Osteoarthritis takes a long time coming; therefore, even with treatment by complementary medicine, it will take a long time going. The main priority is change of diet, for which you need to see a naturopath or nutritionist. You should also take regular supplements including glucosamine sulphate along with calcium, magnesium and vitamin D to promote healthy cartilage cells, again involving the connective tissue and elastic cells of the body. Naturally, the main attitude to develop is going to be flexibility of mind.

In your personal and business life you need to develop natural authority in all that you do, but without being dictatorial or inflexible towards others. You should also aspire towards fulfilling known ambitions but exercise self-control in attaining these goals so as not to impinge upon the will of others. And you need courage, with the ability to take calculated risks.

In reaching your optimum potential, intellectually and physically, try to develop self-control so as not to affect others detrimentally. Always pay attention and learn from life's experiences. Treat yourself at times to those things you really enjoy, and always appreciate art and colour in life – not for their material value or for their fashionable standing but for their beauty.

For both healing and relaxation, you will benefit greatly from massage and from the use of traditional medicine. This is because, once you have reached your optimum mental and physical potential, you will have a raised consciousness that will respond to a more energetic system of medicine. The development of these thoughts and attitudes will prevent the breakdown of cartilage, and in sufferers from osteoarthritis they will assist in the manufacture of more elastic connective tissue cells.

OSTEOPOROSIS

This is a condition where bones become thin and weak and, according to statistics, it occurs more in women than in men. Women lose bone density during the five to ten years after the menopause. However, although only one-in-three women actually have the problem, all women are cajoled into taking HRT in order to prevent bone loss.

∽

Calcium and magnesium with additional vitamins would do the job adequately, but perhaps the revenue attained would be far less than that generated by HRT! Talk to a practitioner in complementary medicine for advice on diet and calcium supplements.

Accepting the progression in a woman's life, from childbearer to matriarch, should not cause displeasure; it is as natural as tomorrow's rising sun. For a woman, an experience of some inner physical conflict, or changes that occur naturally, can often be considered as a 'blessing in disguise' after the event. It may clear the way forward, showing you more precise direction and purpose in life after a period of conflict.

A new dimension exists for the woman after menopause. She has a new role to play, particularly if she has family of her own, as she can be the matriarch to her adult children and grandchildren. All this coincides with the fact that knowledge is gained through experience, and this is the greatest teacher of all. So, see yourself in your meditation or visualisation as the matriarch, or matron, of all you behold. Exercise your newfound abilities for the benefit of your family and for those who seek you out for your wisdom.

PREMENSTRUAL SYNDROME (PMS)

This is a collection of psychological and physical symptoms that affect many women in the days before menstruation. These include mood changes, irritability, depression and anxiety, along with physical symptoms of bloating, headaches and breast tenderness. Many doctors believe this is the result of a drop in progesterone levels in the last half of the menstrual cycle. Prescriptions include both non-hormonal drugs and oral contraceptives, but many doctors favour other supplements, including the B vitamins.

∽

To promote healthy, regular periods, the change in your mental attitudes needs to be long term, not just short term. When stress and trauma appear in your life you need to deal with them very quickly, in an orderly way, and according to your past experiences.

If you have not faced a similar situation before, you will need to draw on tradition, or methods you witnessed your parents using when dealing with the problem (family values being all-important). Truth is central in your day-to-day life. However, in dealing with people in such a traditional manner, you can some-times be a little pedantic and wearisome, due to your insistence upon trivial and unnecessary verbal minutiae. So come straight to the point.

Your style in communication, whether writing or speaking (and this applies both in your younger and older years) must be very clear, but could sometimes lack fire. At times, you can be long-winded in saying all you desire on any possible subject. You need to become a very independent person, business-like, orderly and punctual. You are inclined to dislike flattery or favours, again because of your independence. But independence does not mean isolation, which must be avoided at all cost.

Menstruation does cause feelings of isolation at the time of the period. However, both men and women in relationships can actually be together even when they are apart, supporting each other from a distance, like the columns supporting the roof of a great temple or shrine, such as that of marriage.

PROSTATITIS (see BPH)

PSORIASIS (see also **eczema**)

Psoriasis is a common condition that affects about 2 per cent of the population of the UK. Researchers have found that in psoriasis skin cells replace themselves too quickly, taking a mere four days instead of the twenty-eight days taken in normal skin metabolism. This is why the skin appears red and flaky, with crusty patches. Orthodox medicine has not identified the cause of psoriasis, but in many cases it is stress-induced. It affects young people at puberty and others develop the symptoms at any age between eleven and forty-five.

The condition needs to be treated from within as it concerns the metabolism and over-stimulation of certain cells in the body. Application of topical medication is therefore less successful. Psoriasis patients need to attain calmness and control over any volatile factors in their lives.

Before you developed psoriasis you would have had an innate thirst for knowledge and the need to know the reason behind all things, and this was matched with a keen intellect and profound thinking. However, when the stress started and you had little control of the consequences, there developed a tendency to be a little narrow-minded and critical. Try not to be impatient with others and make efforts to broaden your horizons. Take time to appraise situations, without becoming annoyingly slow, so that your general metabolism is more controlled.

RHEUMATISM (see **arthritis**)

SCHIZOPHRENIA

Schizophrenia is one of the more serious mental disorders. Although disruptive it can be controlled by medication, allowing sufferers to lead near normal, albeit rather subdued, lives.

The main factor to consider in schizophrenia is fear and the feeling of terror that others are against you. Sometimes the patient imagines they are someone else, often someone of importance. These influences can originate from some trauma or distressing event earlier in life. Sufferers from these types of symptoms are often blessed with a strong individuality, which makes them emotionally balanced but also a little intense in their feelings.

If you suffer from schizophrenia there must have been a time in your life when you were called upon to play an important role, whether on the school stage or in your career. At some point, this stress caused you to suffer feelings of inadequacy. You may also have suffered stress and trauma at the hands of an important person, or one you thought was important in subduing your own willpower.

If you have already experienced this, you will benefit from your innate sound judgement in resolving the disputes of those around you through arbitration, stemming from your capacity to see both sides of an argument. This attribute will see you rise to a prominent position in your business career, or at a public level in service to others, perhaps as an administrator or counsellor.

You have a warm heart that responds demonstratively to the oppressed people of the world, and will often give generously, both in time and money, to assist with their plight. Sometimes, in helping others, you hide your inner feelings, allowing your peers to think whatever they please of you. Hiding your feelings in this way will cause eventual outbursts of energy. So it's best to speak quietly about your past worries or traumas with someone who will listen and who you know will not judge you. As I said earlier, fear is often at the root of schizophrenia.

SHINGLES

This is a viral infection that results in a skin rash and flu-like illness and is caused by the chickenpox virus. It only affects people who have previously had chickenpox. The virus hiding in the nerves of the skin becomes active in later life when the immunity to infection weakens.

Homeopathic medicine has many well-proven remedies for this condition and your practitioner will suggest supplements to boost your immune system. The reason you may get shingles is from over-absorption of your own worries and problems, or from being engrossed entirely by one particular direction in life. Sometimes you may appear cold and indifferent to those around you.

There are even times when you feel contempt for those who are less knowledgeable than yourself. These attitudes, however, can lead to inner fears, feelings of inadequacy and loss of nerve. Don't forget that the chickenpox virus hides in the nerves, so strong nerves are essential. Try to be more tolerant of others. Realise that we are not all the same, and that each person you meet is acting out their life according to their own motives.

SKIN CONDITIONS (see **acne**, **eczema** and **psoriasis**)

THYROID DISORDERS

The thyroid gland is located in the lower front portion of the neck and produces hormones that regulate the body's metabolism. This gland can become overactive, producing excess hormones and causing a condition known as hyperthyroidism or it can become underactive, causing hypothyroidism. Drugs can control these conditions and your doctor will request regular monitoring of your progress.

L oneliness and feelings of insecurity can lessen the activity of the thyroid gland, whereas impatience and restlessness and being discontented with life can produce overactivity in the gland. The important factor with thyroid gland disorders is balance in life. In regard to your feelings, both at an emotional and personal level, it is very important for you to be more communicative and demonstrative. You need to learn the body language of others, and accept their feelings, and perhaps their need for physical contact. In this context, try not to be distant from those you are close to.

You have the ability to attain a clear intellect with a substantial interest in the more philosophical aspects of life. Developing flexibility of mind means that you can adapt to changing circumstances and will do well to listen to guidance from others, as well as your inner self and the thoughts that rise within your unconscious mind. During your life you will have to seek out advice from others and you may also be called upon to counsel them. You are equally good at listening and speaking.

You could become a teacher in your chosen field. You just need to build up your confidence, and the fears you have about making changes have to be dispelled. Teachers and singers rarely suffer thyroid symptoms, unless their career is taken from them by other circumstances.

Your powers of concentration can waiver at times, but will be enhanced in the future by you developing a general attitude of acceptance.

Acceptance is based upon the view that all things in life happen for a specific reason to specific people, and this under-standing will lead you to believe that worrying will do little to change the way things are. This renewed way of thinking will apply to your business dealings, and your relationships. A more philosophical attitude will provide you with the power to concentrate upon the realities of a situation. You can then make the correct decisions for the future and for all those concerned in your day-to-day life.

You need to develop a sympathetic approach to others, partic-ularly your family and close friends, offering protection and the best of your help when needed; furthermore it is always best to strive for domestic stability. If you are in business try to learn further skills. This will improve your overall chances of being recognised as managerial material, as you will become known for assisting others.

TINNITUS

Noises and sensations of noises in the ear, possibly caused by a build-up of wax or by fluid imbalance that affects the sound as it is carried to the cochlea for conversion to nerve impulses to the brain for interpretation. Little treatment is available for sufferers.

It is advisable to have your doctor check you out for blockages and fluid build-up, but you should also consider consulting a holistic dental surgeon (see Useful Addresses), as often the teeth are involved, along with the temporal-mandibula joint.

Interaction with people on a day-to-day basis is important for tinnitus sufferers, and communication means more that just the spoken word, or the transference of information by various media, from one to another. Communication is both giving and receiving of information, feelings, thoughts and ideas, at various levels, including listening to your inner self.

ULCERS (peptic)

Peptic ulcers most commonly occur in the walls of the stomach or duodenum when damage to the mucus lining allows stomach acid to erode the underlying tissue. Anti-ulcer drugs are available, but they do not offer an actual cure and therefore have to be taken repeatedly to suppress the symptoms.

Complementary medicine in contrast, addresses the cause and gives dietary and supplement advice to cure the tendency to ulcers, which appear to be stress-induced. The supplements will promote a healthy mucus lining in the stomach.

Patients with ulcers suffer anxiety and worry in both personal and business life. Therefore it is important for you to develop some natural authority in all that you do, but try not to be dictatorial. Ulcer sufferers such as you will often be industrious, with a further attribute of ambition. However, you also need self-control so as not to impinge upon the will of others, and courage, with the ability to take calculated risks.

In reaching the optimum potential intellectually, try to control your own will in a way that won't affect others detrimentally. Always pay attention and learn from life's experiences. Treat yourself at times to those things you really enjoy, and always appreciate the beauty of art (not for its material value, or for its fashionable standing), and colour in life, but do not become addicted. Do not become resentful about others having more material possessions than you as this can create dishonesty and jealousy, which can in turn lead to immoral tendencies.

Your intellectual ability is derived both from inherited qualities and those learnt, not only at an academic level, but also from the lessons of life that come with our day-to-day experiences. Sometimes life appears to be a struggle, in that many projects in your personal life seem fraught with difficulty. However, the struggle is always worth the effort, as the rewards are there at completion. Inner conflict, both of an emotional nature, and sometimes at a business level, will cause you more than normal levels of stress and trauma.

However, conflict does not have to be violent and perhaps we all need to learn that harmony can be obtained through inner conflict by thinking matters through in a very logical manner. Logical thinking, with the addition of a little intuition, will resolve the stress causing your ulcer.

VAGINAL THRUSH

Thrush itself is a very common condition affecting the mouth, the skin under the breasts, the genital area and in particular the vagina. This condition is caused by an overgrowth of yeast called Candida Albicans. This yeast lives naturally in your gut but it can multiply, causing infection and inflammation in the areas mentioned. Topical applications, pessaries and antibiotics are of little use, as by the time vaginal thrush is established the Candida is systemic.

∾

Eat plenty of live natural yoghurt and a good diet of fresh fruit and vegetables for a while, along with some lactobacillus capsules that your naturopathic practitioner can supply. With this condition, we need to look at digestion and the thoughts and attitudes that promote a good digestion.

For thrush sufferers, a harmonious balance in life is essential, and this is especially true regarding the material and the spiritual aspects of life. Your concern for the materialistic should not outweigh your need for spiritual understanding and belief. Having a creed on which to base your life will allow you to balance your material life with the more spiritual aspects that give you both wisdom and understanding of the needs of others. As life goes on, you will be asked more and more to assist those with emotional problems in their lives, because of your under-standing and inner knowledge of solving problems, both at a personal and business level.

It is very important for you to listen to your subconscious mind, or that inner voice that rises within you from time to time, taking care not to repress the intuitive or instinctive knowledge with your rational thought processes. The danger of such repres-sion is that you can become too 'clever' for your own good. You should try to get rid of the rigid attitudes of mind, and allow change to occur naturally, thus revealing the hidden focus that works within all people, leading them to the real purpose of their lives.

The achievement of optimum digestion comes from the balanced energies of devotion and wisdom along with single-mindedness and a purposeful direction in life. Be loyal to those close to you in both personal and business relationships.

VARICOSE VEINS (see **circulatory problems**)

VERRUCAS AND WARTS

A lesion on the skin of viral origin, commonly small and round with a raised rough dry surface. They often plague patients for years and become resistant to topical applications or they re-grow after removal.

Try complementary medicine using Thuja tincture from your homeopathic practitioner or pharmacy, along with potassium elements and supplements to improve your immune system.

As a wart and verrucca sufferer, you have a continual inclination to label or classify things in your life. You always record statements accurately, and place items back in exactly the correct place, as you like your world to be neat, tidy and orderly.

When stress and trauma appear in your life you will deal with them very quickly, in an orderly way and according to your past experiences. Or, if not having faced a similar situation before, you will again draw on traditional methods and past experiences in dealing with the problem. Truth is of the utmost importance in your day-to-day life, and in dealing with people in such a traditional manner you can sometimes be a little pedantic and wearisome. Do not insist upon trivial and unnecessary verbal minutiae. Just say it as quickly and accurately as possible. Concentration on small details will allow your little warts to proliferate.

VERTIGO (see **dizziness** and **Menière's syndrome**)

NOTE

The above thoughts, attributes and attitudes have been drawn from our database of over 4000 case histories. There will be people who do not relate totally to the written text, as all patients are different in their personalities. Patients may contact the author for individual assessments and further information (see page 195).

Useful Addresses

For professional advice and information on products mentioned in this book, contact the following companies who will provide names of qualified practitioners in your area. These companies do not supply the general public without referral.

For vitamins, digestive enzymes, mineral supplements and advice on qualified practitioners, consult:

Metagenics UK,
16a St Mary's Street,
Wallingford,
Oxon OX10 0EW,
UK.

Metagenics Inc. (USA),
100 Avenida La Pata,
San Clemente,
CA 92673,
USA.

For elemental celloids, herbal remedies and professional advice:

Blackmores UK,
Willow Tree Marina,
West Quay Drive,
Yeading,
Middlesex UB4 9TB,
UK.

Blackmores (Australia),
Toll-free Australia-wide 1800 803 760.

For biochemic tissue salts based upon the Dr Schuessler system of medicine and Dr Bach flower essences, ask at most health stores worldwide.

For lists of professional homeopaths, herbalists, osteopaths and chiropractors, and advice on complementary medicine, including meditation and yoga, in the UK, write to:

The Institute for Complementary Medicine,
PO Box 194,
London SE16 1QZ.

For information on holistic dentistry contact:

The International Academy of Oral Medicine Toxicology,
Dr Anthony Newman,
72 Harley Street,
London W1N 1AC.

For personal consultations and appointments or computerised optimum potential reports and information on lectures and seminars write (enclosing a stamped addressed envelope) to:

Keith Mason,
Hope Cottage,
Breamore,
Fordingbridge,
Hampshire SP6 2BX,
UK.

FURTHER READING

Medicine for the 21st Century by Keith Mason (Element Books)

The New Biology by Robert Augros and George Stanciu (Random House)

The Cosmic Blueprint by Paul Davies (Touchstone)

Superstrings by Paul Davies and Julian Brown (Cambridge University Press)

Beyond Supernature by Dr Lyall Watson (Hodder and Stoughton)

The Secret Life of Plants by Peter Tompkins and Christopher Bird (Penguin Book)

CHECKLIST OF COMMON AILMENTS

Condition	Possible causes	Possible cures	Page
Acne	Unwelcome changes	Love yourself – be assertive	81
Addictions	Accepting obstacles	Respond to life's challenges	82
Agoraphobia	Fear of love	Learn through love	84
Anaemia	Demanding too much from life	Look at the needs of others	85
Anger	Bitterness	Inner peace	86
Angina	Inflexibility and worry	Adaptability	87
Anorexia	Stress and trauma	Self-confidence	89
Anxiety	Inner apprehension	Selflessness	92
Arthritis	Lack of courage to change	Determination	96
Asthma	Fear and loneliness	Communication – speak out	97
Back pain	Complacency, being manipulative	Be responsible	99
Bed-wetting	Guilt	Fluid thought, harmony	100
Bladder problems	Missed opportunities	Take heed	101
Blood pressure, high	Stubborn and dogmatic	Show initiative, take more risks	102
Blood pressure, low	Inconsistency	Flexible thoughts	104
BPH	Looking back at past	Use wisdom to look forward	105
Breast lumps	Non-acceptance of change	Evolve, set goals and aspirations	106
Bronchitis	Overprotective	Pliability	108
Cancer	Shock or trauma	Visualise the change	110
Catarrh	Self-righteous	Step back	114
Change of life	Non-acceptance	New beginnings	115
Childhood infections	Weak immunity	Stronger constitution	116
Chronic fatigue syndrome	Thwarted ambition	Use innate talents	118
Circulatory problems	Lack of elasticity	Buoyancy, bending	120

Condition	Possible causes	Possible cures	Page
Colds, coughs and influenza	Intolerance	Contentment	121
Colic	Suspicion	Inevitable changes	122
Constipation	Blocked emotions	Harmonious balance	123
COPD	No expression	Speak your mind	125
Corpulence	Obsessive	Face the challenge	126
Cramp	Restrictive practices	Develop imagination	127
Crohn's disease	Inadequacies	Listen to inner self	128
Cystitis	Rigid views	Broaden horizons	130
Deafness	Resignation	Innovation	131
Debility	Unjustifiable stress	Strong will	132
Delirium	Repeated mistakes	Rational thinking	133
Depression	Lack of endurance	Initiative and determination	134
Despondency	Overburdened	Planning and contingencies	137
Diabetes	Intellectual stress	Creativity and perception	139
Diarrhoea	Lack of concentration	Control skills	140
Diverticulitis	Awkwardness	Less intransigence	141
Dizziness	Ignore advice	Listen to yourself	142
Dry eye	Contradictory	Contemplation	143
Dyspepsia	Crisis to crisis	Better judgements	144
Eczema	Muddled life	More accuracy	145
Epilepsy	Aloofness	Logic and creative thinking	147
Fear	Excessive devotion	Patience and understanding	148
Fevers	Lack of trust	Build confidence	149
Fibroids	Rigidity	Expand boundaries	150
Fibromyalgia	Negative thoughts	Take calculated risks	151
Gallstones	Pent-up anger	Address causes	154
Glandular fever	Mental exertion	Plan and think ahead	154
Glaucoma	Distasteful happenings	Less impetuosity	155
Gout	Reaping what's been sown	Self-control	156
Grief	Hiding pain	Tell a friend	157
Haemorrhoids	Headstrong, unbending	Sharpen wit	158
Hayfever	Impatience	Precision	159
Heart conditions	Emotional disorder	Understand others	161
Heartburn	Avoid anger	Accept change	163
Heavy periods	Clumsy manner	Let ideas proliferate	164
Hernias	Self-centred	Listen to others	166
Hypertension	Lack of direction	Self-will	166
Hysteria	Lack of resolve	Take initiative	167
Impotence	Too comfortable	Take on new projects	168
Insomnia	Accept others' ways	Step back and review	169

Condition	Possible causes	Possible cures	Page
Irritable bowel syndrome	Unwelcome change	Change routine	170
Kidney problems	Lack of willpower	Self-reliance	172
Lethargy	Resignation	Creation and innovation	174
Meniere's syndrome	Singularity of thought	Widen horizons	175
Migraines	Discrimination	Creative arts	176
Neuralgia	Obstinacy	Adaptability	178
Obsessions	Pristine attitudes	Multiple activities	179
Osteoarthritis	Long-term inflexibility	Self-control	180
Osteoporosis	Holding back emotions	Accept progression	181
Premenstrual syndrome	Lack of accuracy	Come to the point	182
Psoriasis	Volatile thoughts	Calmness	183
Schizophrenia	Never self-satisfied	Inner judgements	184
Shingles	Inner fears	Tolerance	185
Thyroid disorders	Insecurity, loneliness	Demonstrative	186
Tinnitus	Lack of interaction	Communicate ideas	188
Ulcers	Lack of authority	Develop self-control	188
Vaginal thrush	Irrational at times	Give good counsel	190
Verrucas and warts	Hanging on to past	Look ahead	191

GET YOUR OWN COMPUTERISED HEALTH STATUS REPORT

My years of research into the mind–body links between common illnesses, thoughts and attitudes have culminated in a research database and computer program. I now use this program to assist people from all over the world in their well-being and healthcare. Applicants simply complete and return a small questionnaire by ticking twelve boxes, and include their full name and date of birth and the country in which they were born. This information is then entered into my computer which produces a totally individual report, giving nine categories of attributes and aspirations with individual headings in order, from the strongest to the weakest areas of their character, which can possibly affect their health. In addition, the program produces advice on actions and thoughts to be taken when affected by stress and, if applicable, the type of diet needed to assist the patient's physical well-being.

For further information or a questionnaire, write (enclosing a stamped addressed envelope) to:

Keith Mason,
Hope Cottage,
Breamore,
Fordingbridge,
Hampshire SP6 2BX,
UK.

INDEX

Piatkus Books

If you have enjoyed reading this book, you may be interested in other titles published by Piatkus. These include:

As I See It: A psychic's guide to developing your healing and sensing abilities   Betty F. Balcombe

Awakening To Change: A guide to self-empowerment in the new millennium   Soozi Holbeche

Care Of The Soul: How to add depth and meaning to your everyday life   Thomas Moore

Child Of Eternity, A: An extraordinary girl's message from the world beyond   Adriana Rocha and Kristi Jorde

Full Catastrophe Living: How to cope with stress, pain and illness using mindfulness meditation   Jon Kabat-Zinn

Handbook For The Soul: A collection of writings from over 30 celebrated spiritual writers   Richard Clarkson and Benjamin Shields (eds.)

How Meditation Heals: A practical guide to the power of meditation to heal common ailments and emotional problems   Eric Harrison

Journey Of Self-Discovery: How to work with the energies of chakras and archetypes   Ambika Wauters

Karma And Reincarnation: The key to spiritual evolution and enlightenment   Dr Hiroshi Motoyama

Light Up Your Life: And discover your true purpose and potential   Diana Cooper

Meditation For Every Day: Includes over 100 inspiring meditations for busy people   Bill Anderton

Message Of Love, A: A channelled guide to our future   Ruth White

Messenger, The: The journey of a spiritual teacher   Geoff Boltwood

Mindfulness Meditation For Everyday Life   Jon Kabat-Zinn

Reiki For Common Ailments: A practical guide to healing   Mari Hall

River Of Life, The: A guide to your spiritual journey   Ruth White

Stepping Into The Magic: A new approach to everyday life   Gill Edwards

Teach Yourself To Meditate: Over 20 simple exercises for peace, health and clarity of mind   Eric Harrison

Three Minute Meditator, The: 30 simple ways to relax and unwind   David Harp with Nina Feldman
Time For Healing, A: The journey to wholeness   Eddie and Debbie Shapiro
Time For Transformation, A: How to awaken to your soul's purpose and claim your power   Diana Cooper
Toward A Meaningful Life: A wisdom of the Rebbe Menachem Mendel Schneersohn   Simon Jacobson (ed.)
Transform Your Life: A step-by-step programme for change   Diana Cooper
Working With Guides And Angels   Ruth White
Working With Your Chakras   Ruth White
Your Body Speaks Your Mind: Understand how your thoughts and emotions affect your health   Debbie Shapiro
Your Mind's Eye: How to heal yourself and release your potential through creative visualisation   Rachel Charles

For a free brochure with our complete list of titles, please write to:

Piatkus Books
5 Windmill Street
London W1P 1HF

Tel: 020 7631 0710
Email: info@piatkus.co.uk
Website: www.piatkus.co.uk